Fun and Easy! English-Spanish Picture Dictionary

Ordering Information: Quantity sales. Special discounts are available on quantity purchases by corporations, associations, and others. For details, contact the publisher at the email address above.

Printed in the United States of America

ISBN-13:979-11-88195-24-4

Tabla de Contenido

BODY (CUERPO)

Head (Cabeza)
Face (Cara)
Neck (Cuello)
Chest (Pecho)
Shoulder (Hombro)
Waist (Cintura)
Arm(Brazo)
Elbow(Codo)
Pelvis
Abdomen
Hand (Mano)
Leg (Pierna)
Thigh (Muslo)
Knee (Rodilla)
Foot(Pie)
Sheen(Espinilla)

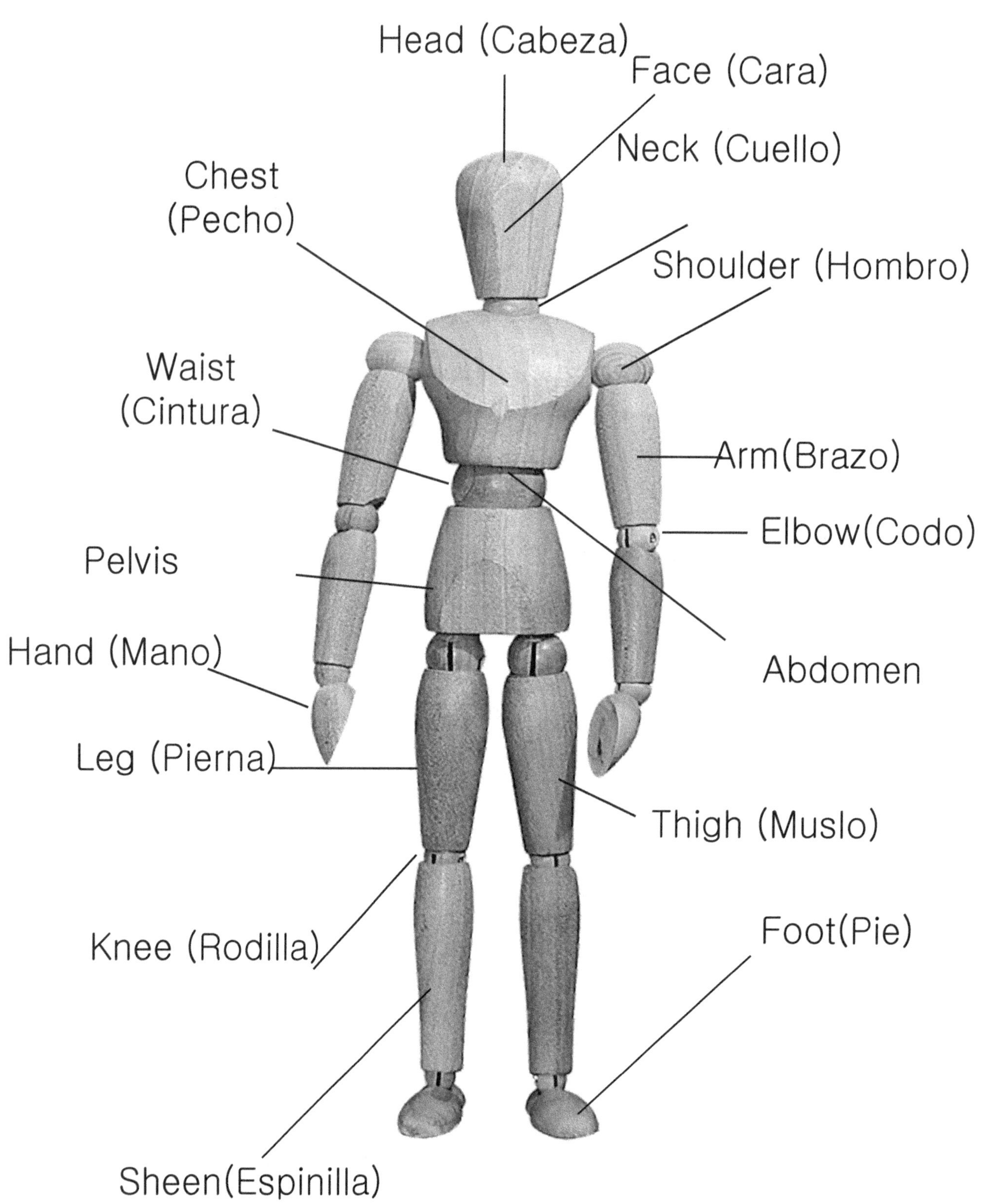

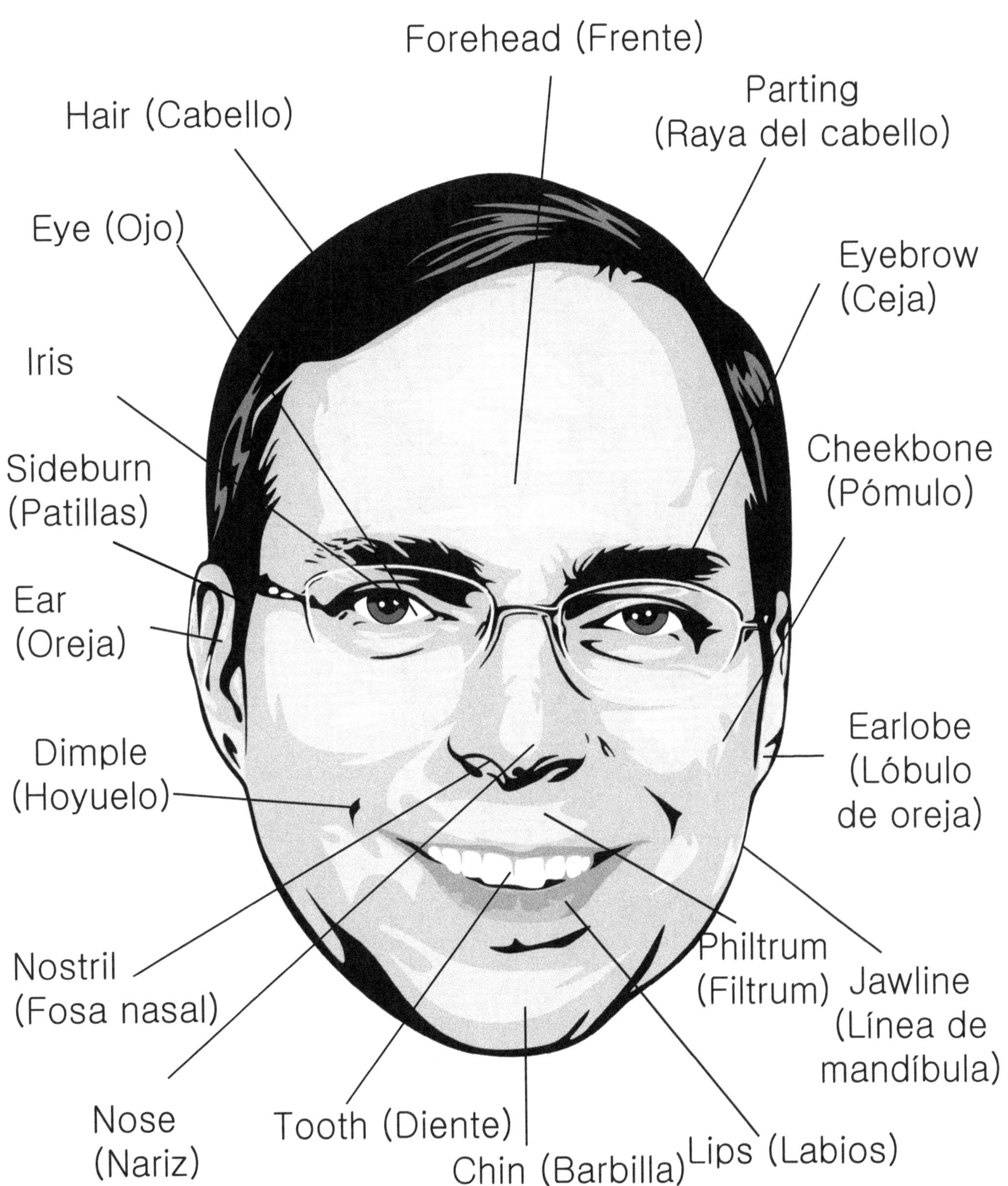

Forehead (Frente)
Parting (Raya del cabello)
Hair (Cabello)
Eyebrow (Ceja)
Eye (Ojo)
Iris
Cheekbone (Pómulo)
Sideburn (Patillas)
Ear (Oreja)
Earlobe (Lóbulo de oreja)
Dimple (Hoyuelo)
Philtrum (Filtrum)
Jawline (Línea de mandíbula)
Nostril (Fosa nasal)
Nose (Nariz)
Tooth (Diente)
Chin (Barbilla)
Lips (Labios)

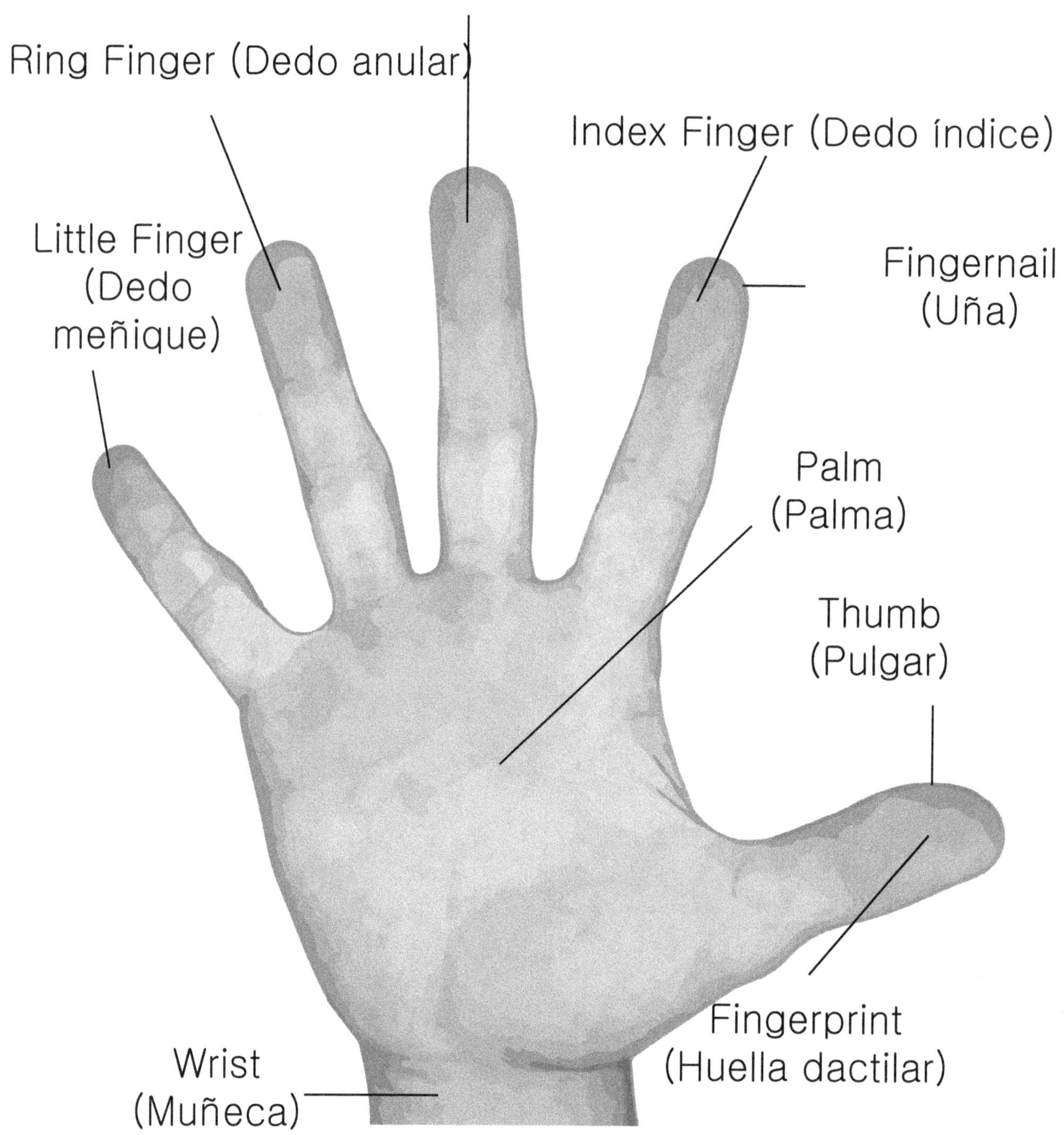

Middle Finger (Dedo medio)
Ring Finger (Dedo anular)
Index Finger (Dedo índice)
Little Finger (Dedo meñique)
Fingernail (Uña)
Palm (Palma)
Thumb (Pulgar)
Wrist (Muñeca)
Fingerprint (Huella dactilar)

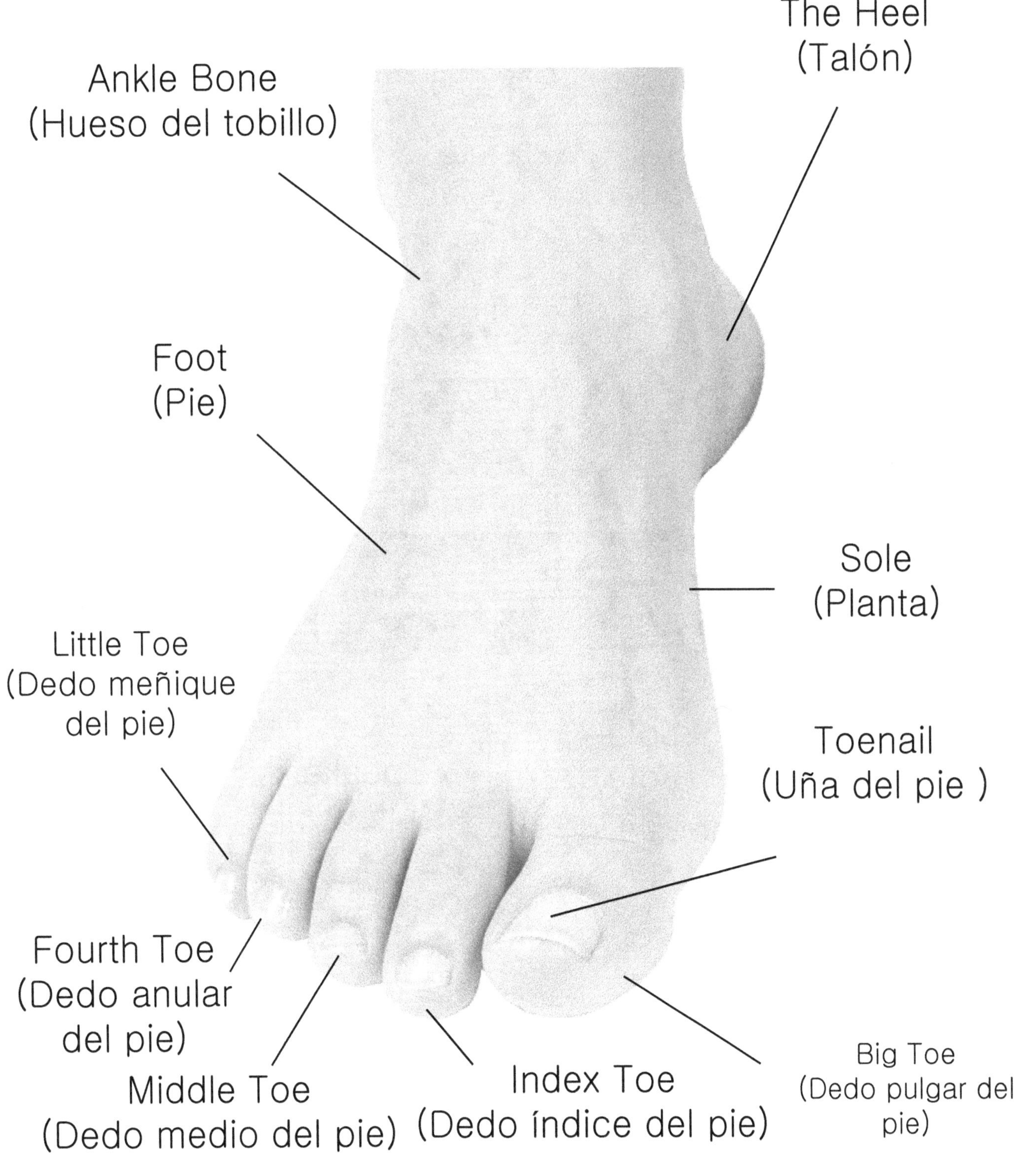

The Heel
(Talón)
Ankle Bone
(Hueso del tobillo)
Foot
(Pie)
Sole
(Planta)
Little Toe
(Dedo meñique
del pie)
Toenail
(Uña del pie)
Fourth Toe
(Dedo anular
del pie)
Middle Toe
(Dedo medio del pie)
Index Toe
(Dedo índice del pie)
Big Toe
(Dedo pulgar del
pie)

HOME (CASA)

Grandfather Clock
(Reloj de abuelo)
Painting
(Pintura)
Television
(Televisión)
Drawer
(Cajón)
Table Lamp
(Lámpara de mesa)
Photo Frame
(Marco de
la foto)
Telephone
(Teléfono)
Sofa
(Sofá)
Speaker
(Altavoz)
Bookshelf
(Estante
para libros)
Fireplace
(Chimenea)

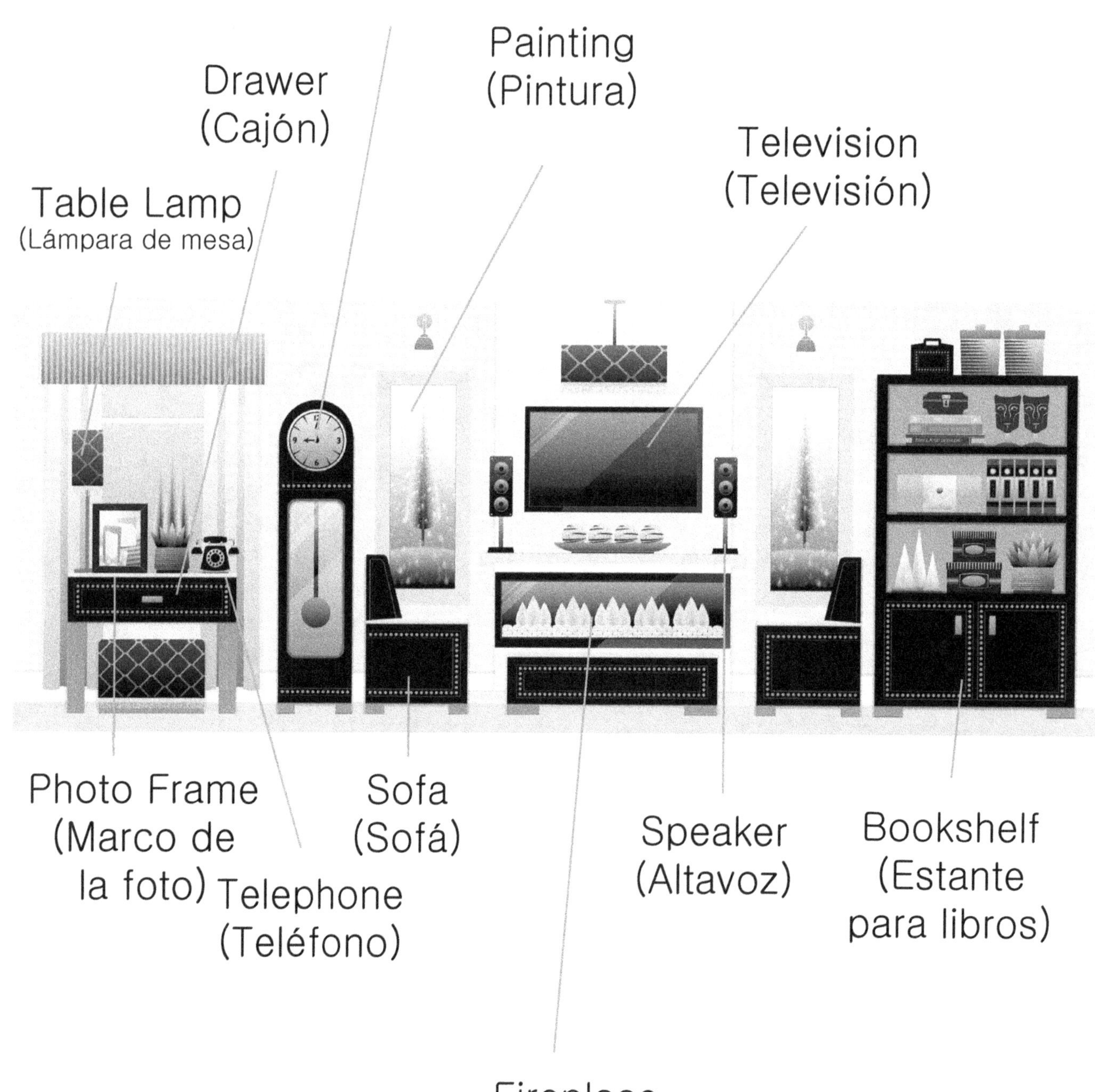

Window
(Ventana)

Wall Mirror
(Espejo de pared)

Bird Cage
(Jaula de pájaros)

Chair
(Silla)

Wooden Floor
(Suelo de madera)

Flower Pot
(Maceta)

Curtain
(Cortina)

Rug
(Alfombra)

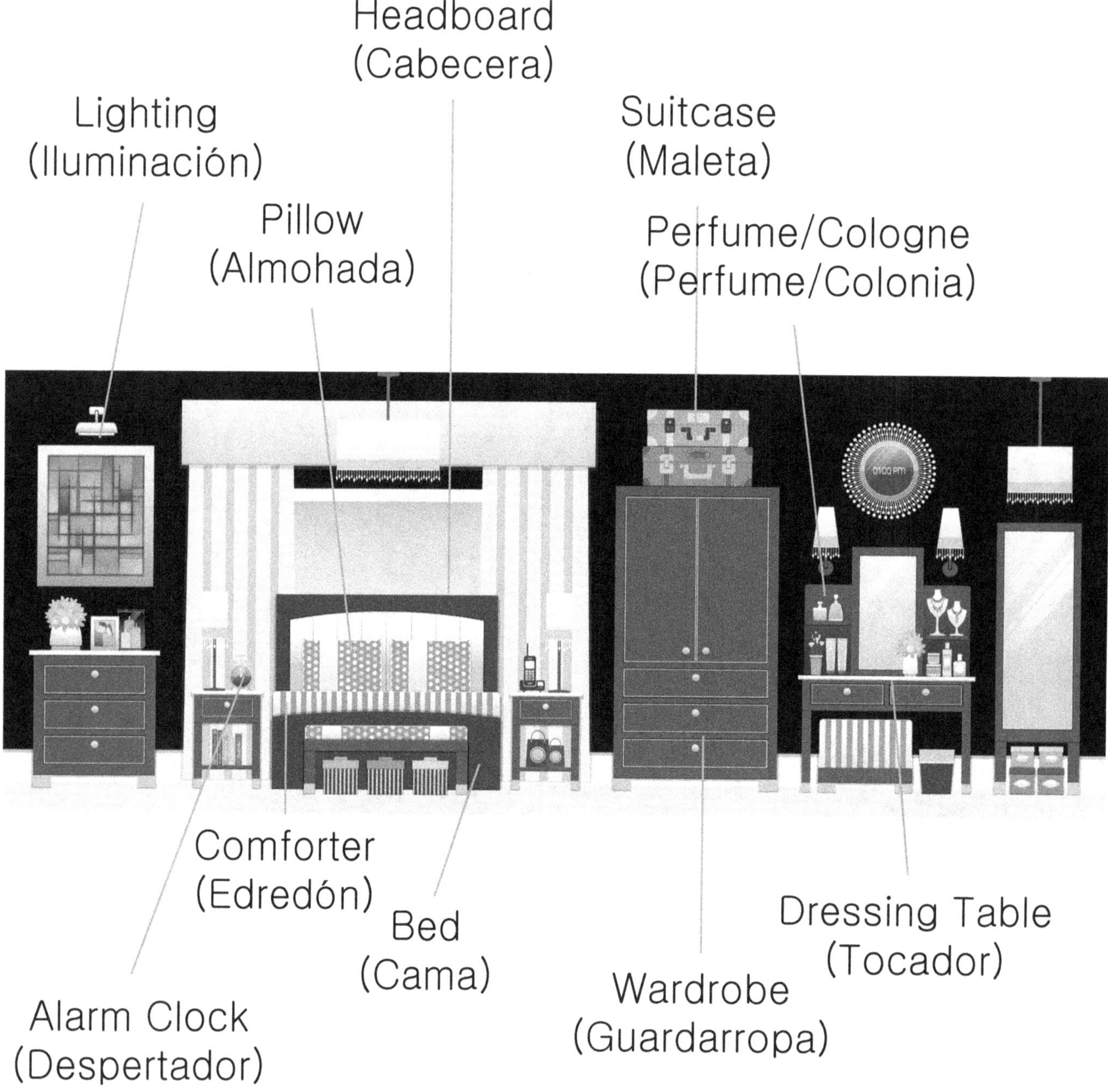

Headboard
(Cabecera)
Lighting
(Iluminación)
Pillow
(Almohada)
Suitcase
(Maleta)
Perfume/Cologne
(Perfume/Colonia)
Comforter
(Edredón)
Bed
(Cama)
Alarm Clock
(Despertador)
Wardrobe
(Guardarropa)
Dressing Table
(Tocador)

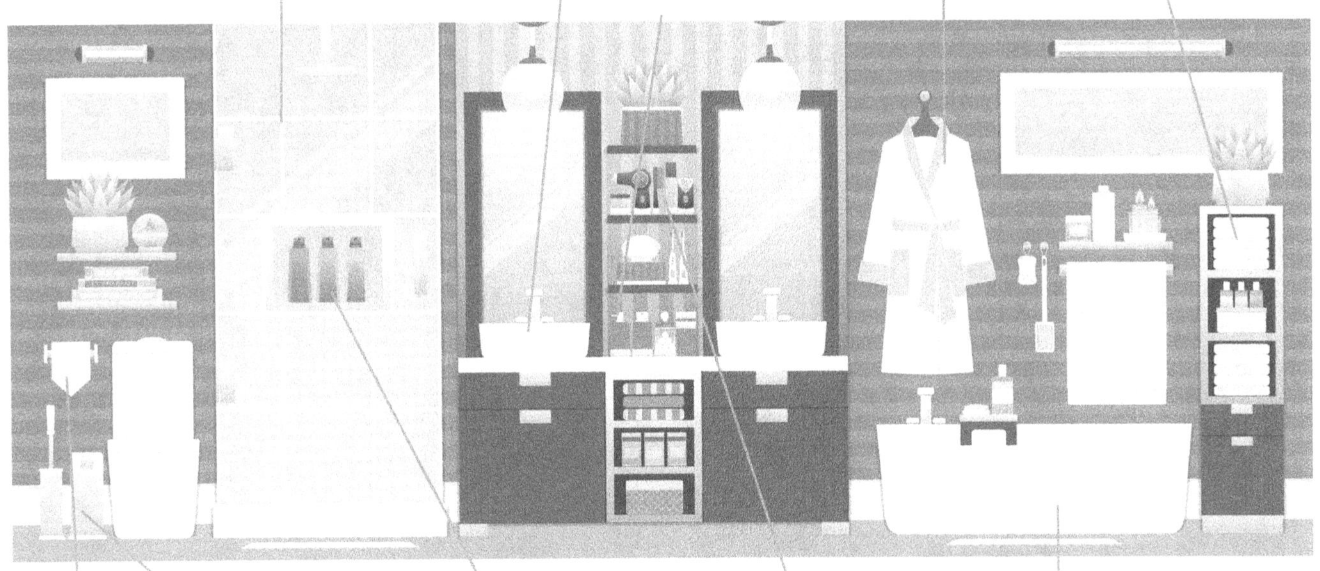

Shoewr Stall
(Cabina de ducha)
Basin
(Lavabo)
Bathrobe
(Bata de baño)
Towel
(Toalla)
Toothbursh/Toothpaste
(Cepillo de dientes/pasta de dientes)
Scale
(Báscula)
Soap/Shampoo/
Body Wash
(Jabón/champú/
jabon para el cuerpo)
Bathtub
(Bañera)
Toilet Paper
(Papel higienico)
Razor/Shaver
(Maquinilla de afeitar)

Spatula/Rice Paddle/
Cutting Board/Knife
(Espátula / Arroz Paddle /
Placa de corte / cuchillo)

Exhaust Fan
(Extractor de aire)

Refrigerator
(Refrigerador)

Spice Jar
(Tarro de especias)

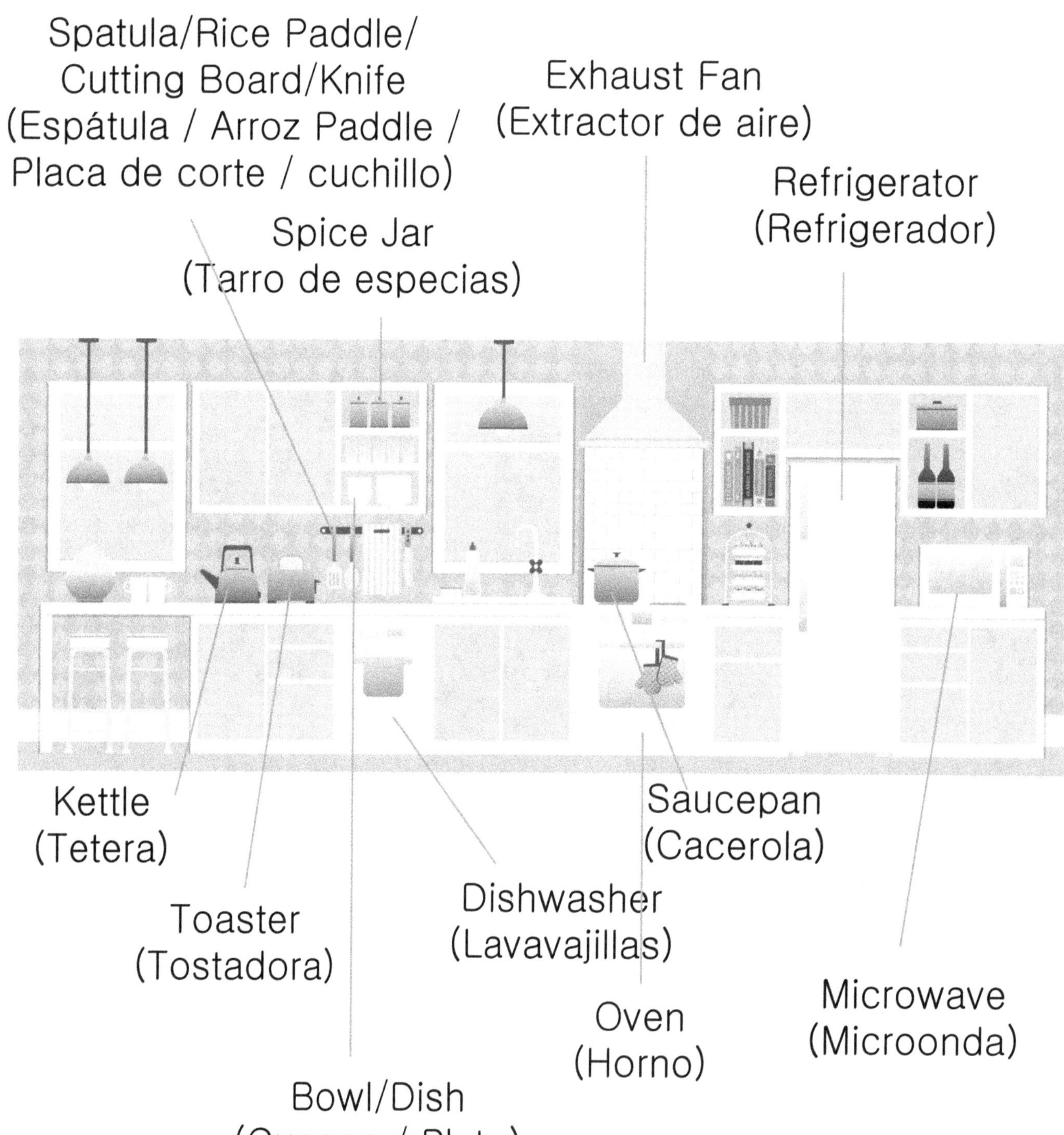

Kettle
(Tetera)

Saucepan
(Cacerola)

Toaster
(Tostadora)

Dishwasher
(Lavavajillas)

Oven
(Horno)

Microwave
(Microonda)

Bowl/Dish
(Cuenco / Plato)

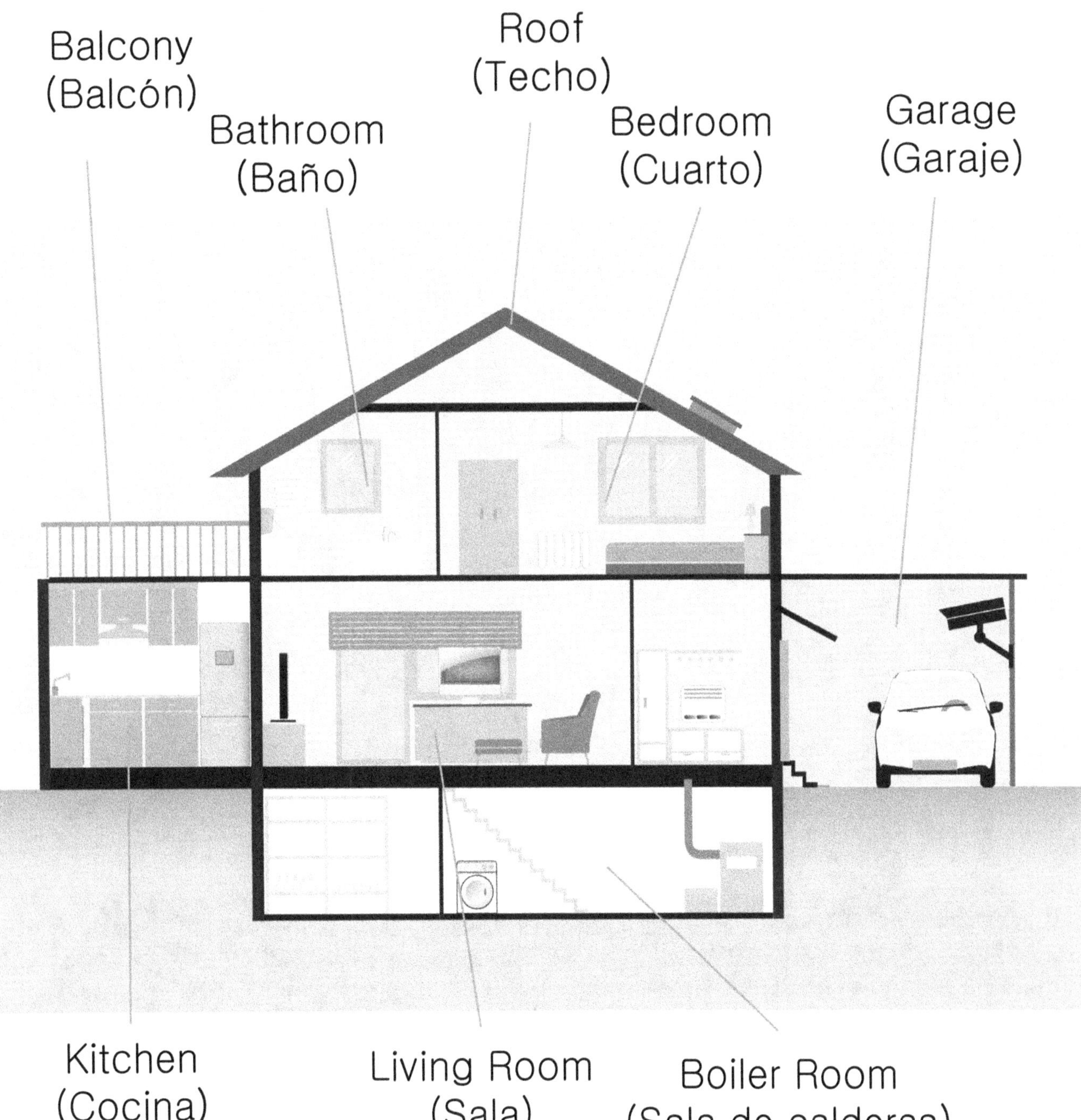

Balcony
(Balcón)
Bathroom
(Baño)
Roof
(Techo)
Bedroom
(Cuarto)
Garage
(Garaje)
Kitchen
(Cocina)
Living Room
(Sala)
Boiler Room
(Sala de calderas)

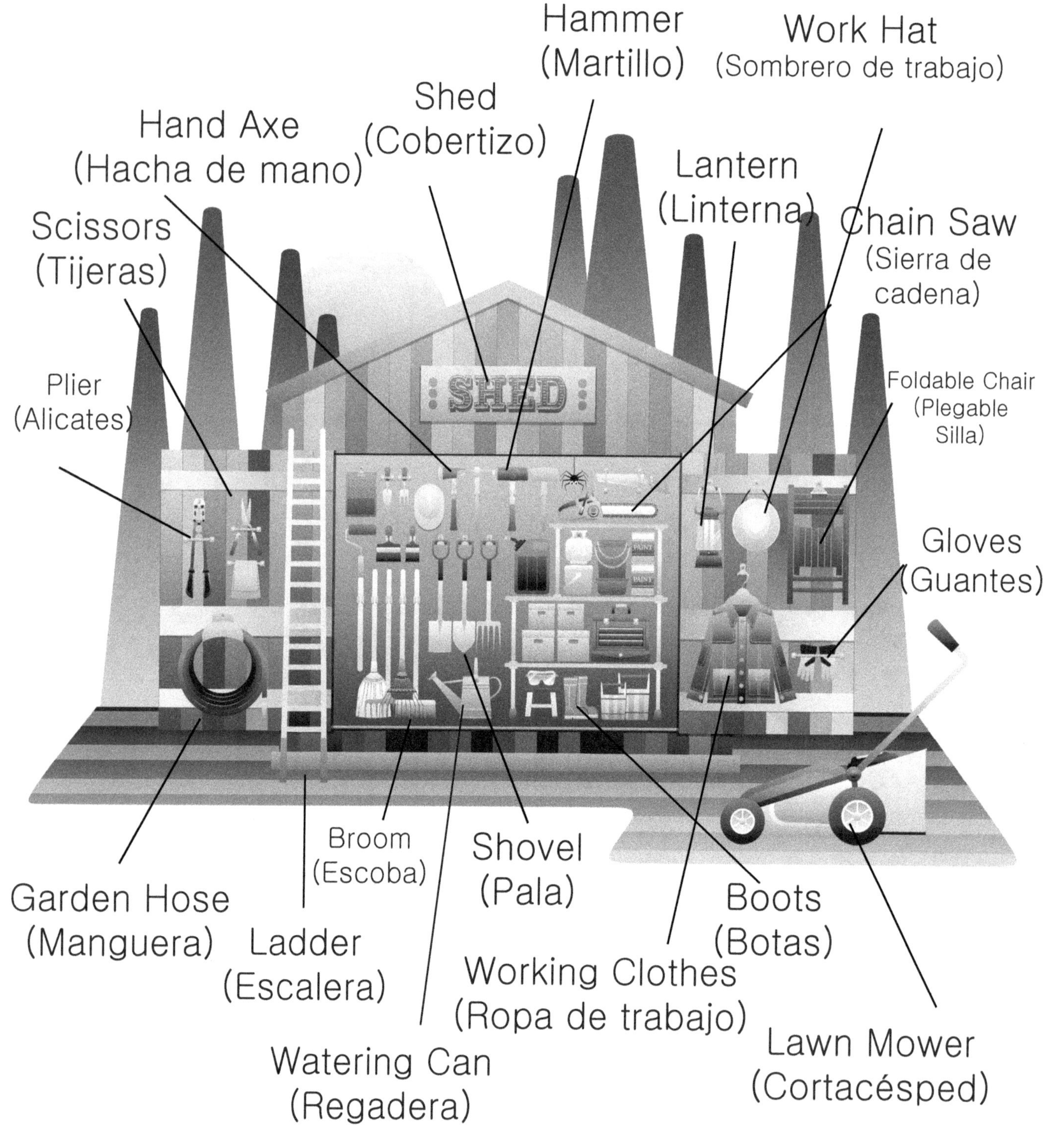

Hammer
(Martillo)
Work Hat
(Sombrero de trabajo)
Shed
(Cobertizo)
Hand Axe
(Hacha de mano)
Lantern
(Linterna)
Scissors
(Tijeras)
Chain Saw
(Sierra de cadena)
Plier
(Alicates)
SHED
Foldable Chair
(Plegable Silla)
Gloves
(Guantes)
Garden Hose
(Manguera)
Ladder
(Escalera)
Broom
(Escoba)
Shovel
(Pala)
Boots
(Botas)
Working Clothes
(Ropa de trabajo)
Watering Can
(Regadera)
Lawn Mower
(Cortacésped)

HOUSEHOLD ITEMS (Artículos para el hogar)

Cell Phone
(Teléfono móvil)

Radio (Radio)

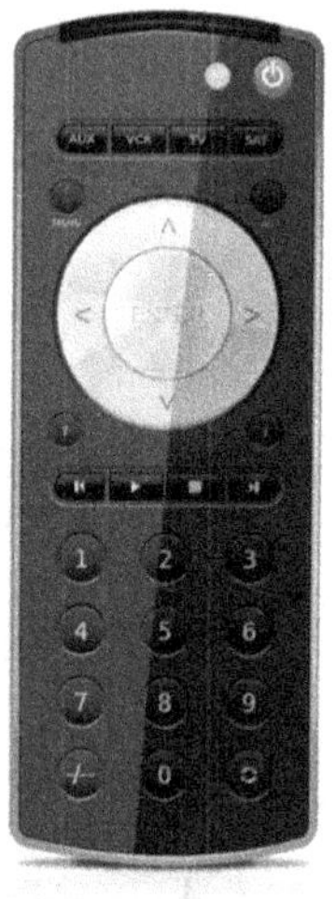

Remote Controller
(Control remoto)

Wallet (Billetera)

Washboard (Lavadero)

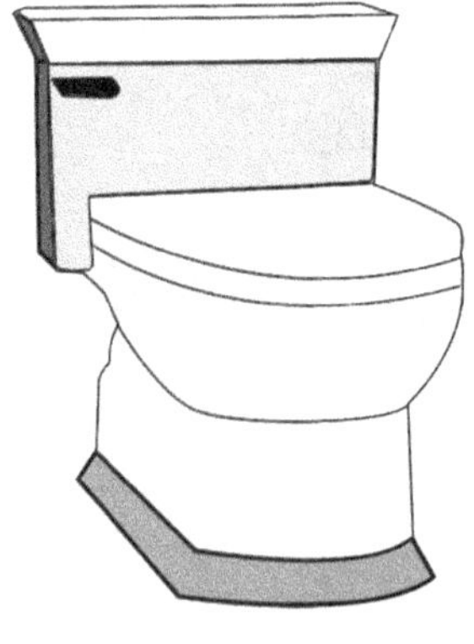

Toilet (Váter)

SUPERMARKET (SUPERMERCADO)

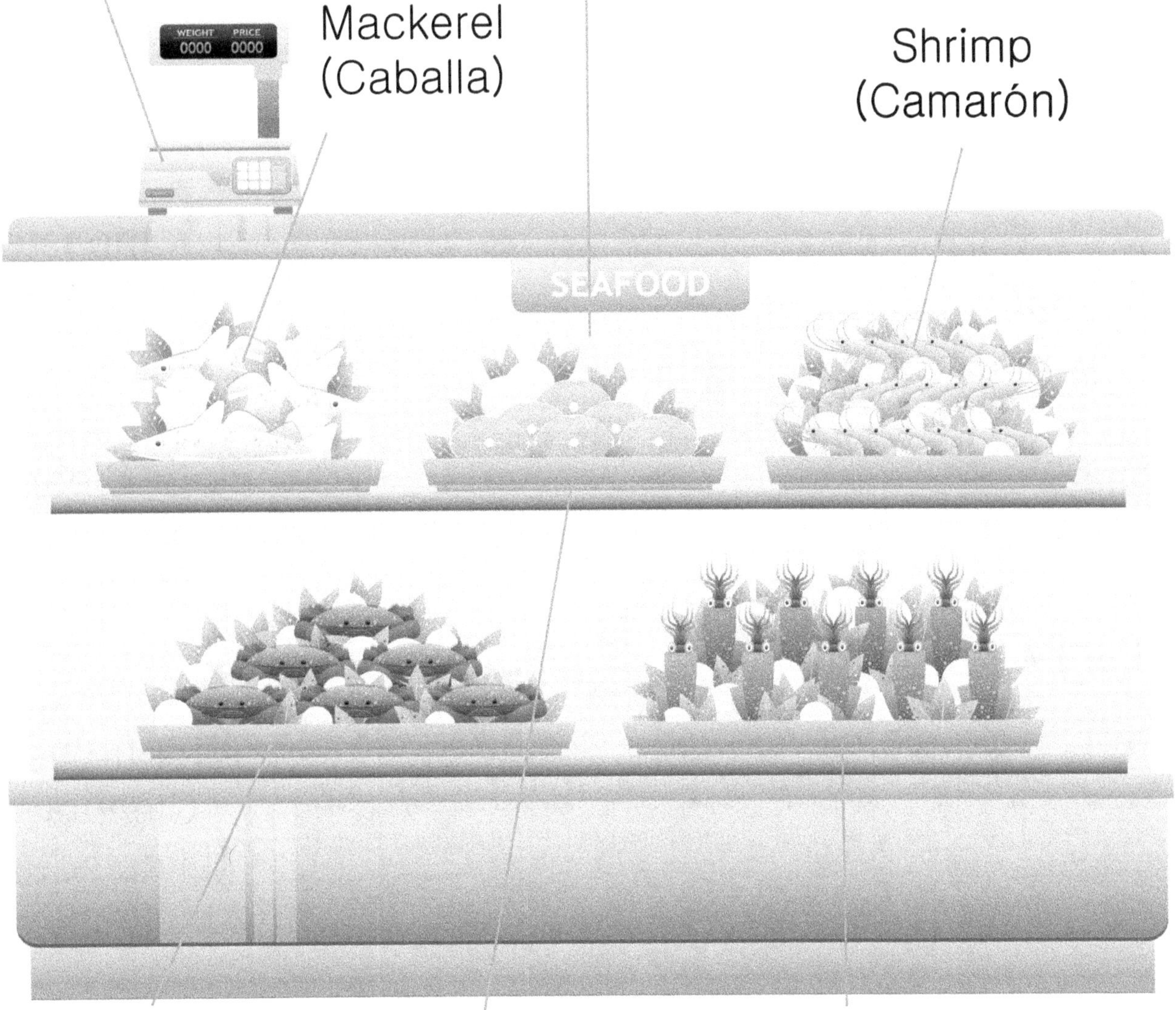

Shampoo / Conditioner
(Champú / Acondicionador)
Bodywash
(Gel de ducha)
SHAMPOO
CONDITIONER
SHAMPOO
CONDITIONER
SHOWER GEL
SHOWER GEL
SHOWER GEL
SHOWER GEL
Toothpaste
(Pasta dental)
Soap
(Jabón)
SOAP
SOAP
SOAP
SOAP
SOAP
SOAP
FACEWASH
FACEWASH
FACEWASH
HANDWASH
HANDWASH
HANDWASH
TOOTHPASTE
TOOTHPASTE
TOOTHPASTE
TOOTHPASTE
Floor Cleaner
(Limpiador de pisos)
Dish Soap
(Jabón de plato)
DISHWASH
DISHWASH
DISHWASH
FLOOR CLEANER
FLOOR CLEANER
ALL PURPOSE CLEANER
ALL PURPOSE CLEANER
ALL PURPOSE CLEANER
All-Purpsoe Cleaner
(Limpiador multiuso)
LAUNDRY
LAUNDRY
LAUNDRY
LAUNDRY
BLEACH
BLEACH
Laundry Detergent
(Detergente de lavandería)
Bleach
(Blanqueador)

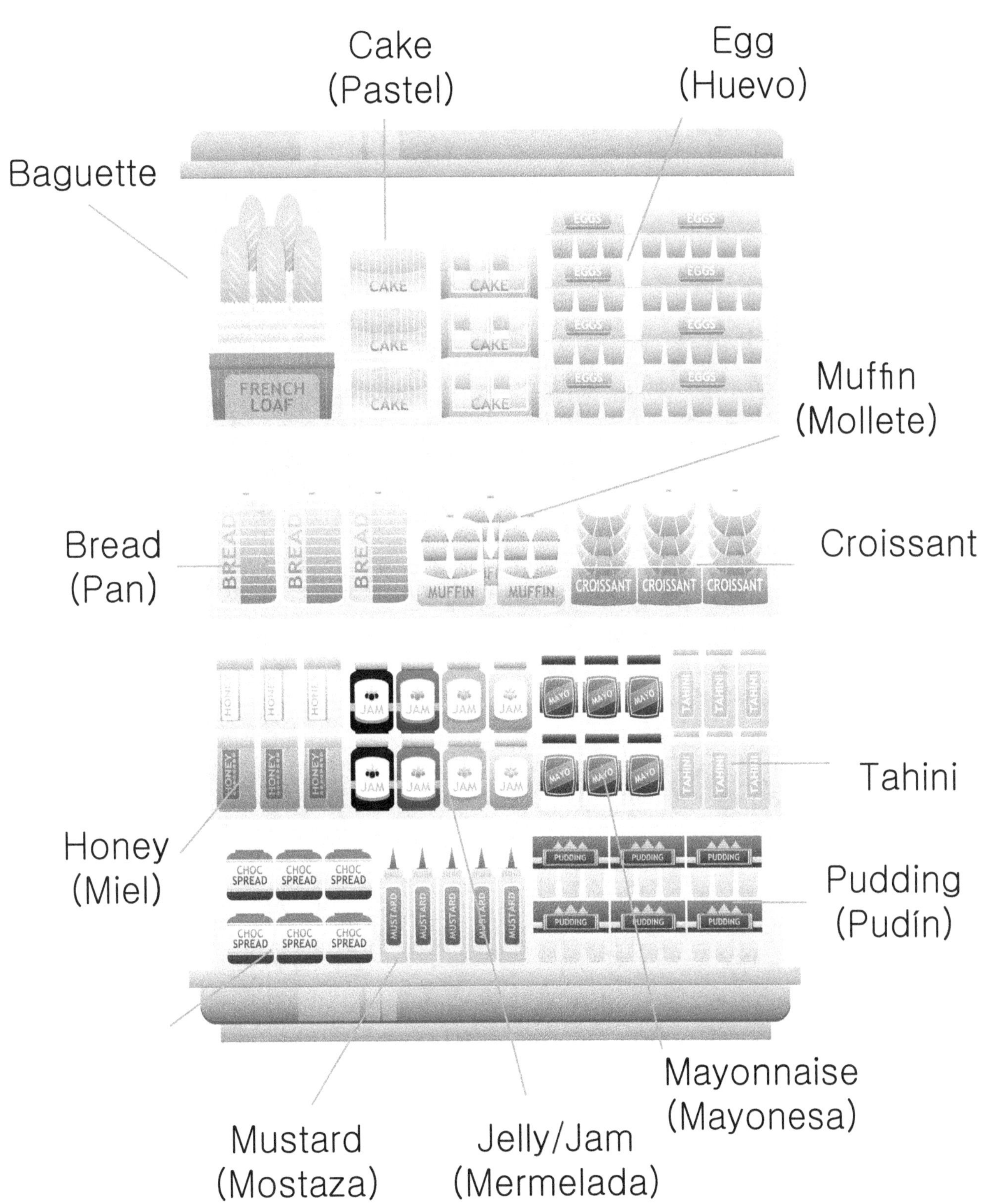

Cake
(Pastel)
Egg
(Huevo)
Baguette
CAKE
CAKE
CAKE
CAKE
CAKE
CAKE
EGGS
EGGS
EGGS
EGGS
EGGS
EGGS
EGGS
EGGS
FRENCH LOAF
Muffin
(Mollete)
Bread
(Pan)
BREAD
BREAD
BREAD
MUFFIN
MUFFIN
CROISSANT
CROISSANT
CROISSANT
Croissant
HONEY
HONEY
HONEY
JAM
JAM
JAM
JAM
JAM
JAM
JAM
JAM
MAYO
MAYO
MAYO
MAYO
MAYO
MAYO
TAHINI
TAHINI
TAHINI
TAHINI
TAHINI
TAHINI
Tahini
Honey
(Miel)
CHOC SPREAD
CHOC SPREAD
CHOC SPREAD
CHOC SPREAD
CHOC SPREAD
CHOC SPREAD
MUSTARD
MUSTARD
MUSTARD
MUSTARD
MUSTARD
PUDDING
PUDDING
PUDDING
PUDDING
PUDDING
PUDDING
Pudding
(Pudín)
Mayonnaise
(Mayonesa)
Mustard
(Mostaza)
Jelly/Jam
(Mermelada)

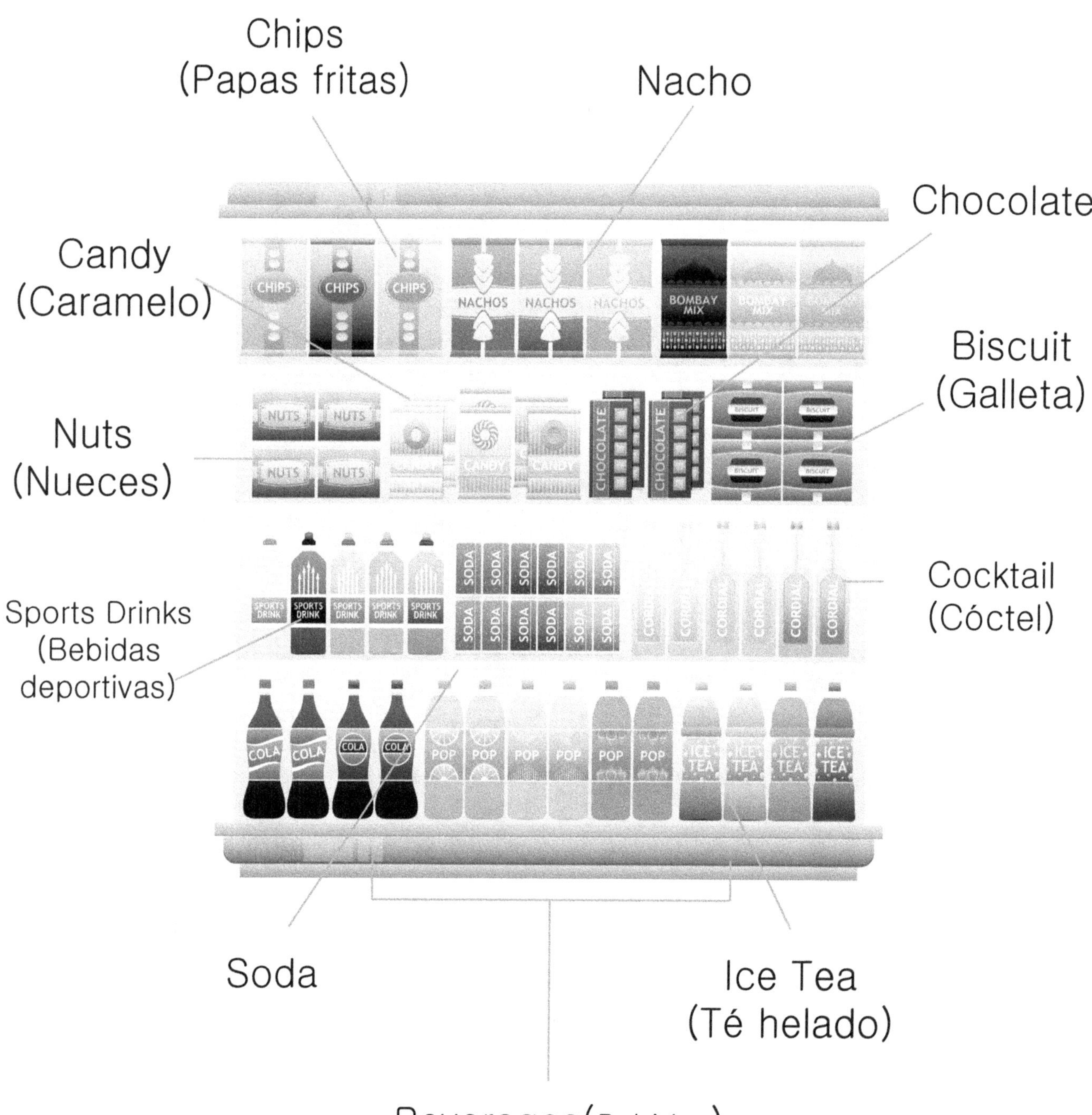

Chips
(Papas fritas)
Nacho
Chocolate
Candy
(Caramelo)
Biscuit
(Galleta)
Nuts
(Nueces)
Sports Drinks
(Bebidas
deportivas)
Cocktail
(Cóctel)
Soda
Ice Tea
(Té helado)
Beverages(Bebidas)
CHIPS
CHIPS
CHIPS
NACHOS
NACHOS
NACHOS
BOMBAY MIX
BOMBAY MIX
NUTS
NUTS
NUTS
NUTS
CANDY
CANDY
CHOCOLATE
CHOCOLATE
BISCUIT
BISCUIT
BISCUIT
BISCUIT
SPORTS DRINK
SPORTS DRINK
SPORTS DRINK
SPORTS DRINK
SPORTS DRINK
SODA
SODA
SODA
SODA
SODA
SODA
SODA
SODA
SODA
SODA
SODA
SODA
CORDIAL
CORDIAL
CORDIAL
CORDIAL
CORDIAL
CORDIAL
COLA
COLA
COLA
COLA
POP
POP
POP
POP
POP
POP
ICE TEA
ICE TEA
ICE TEA
ICE TEA

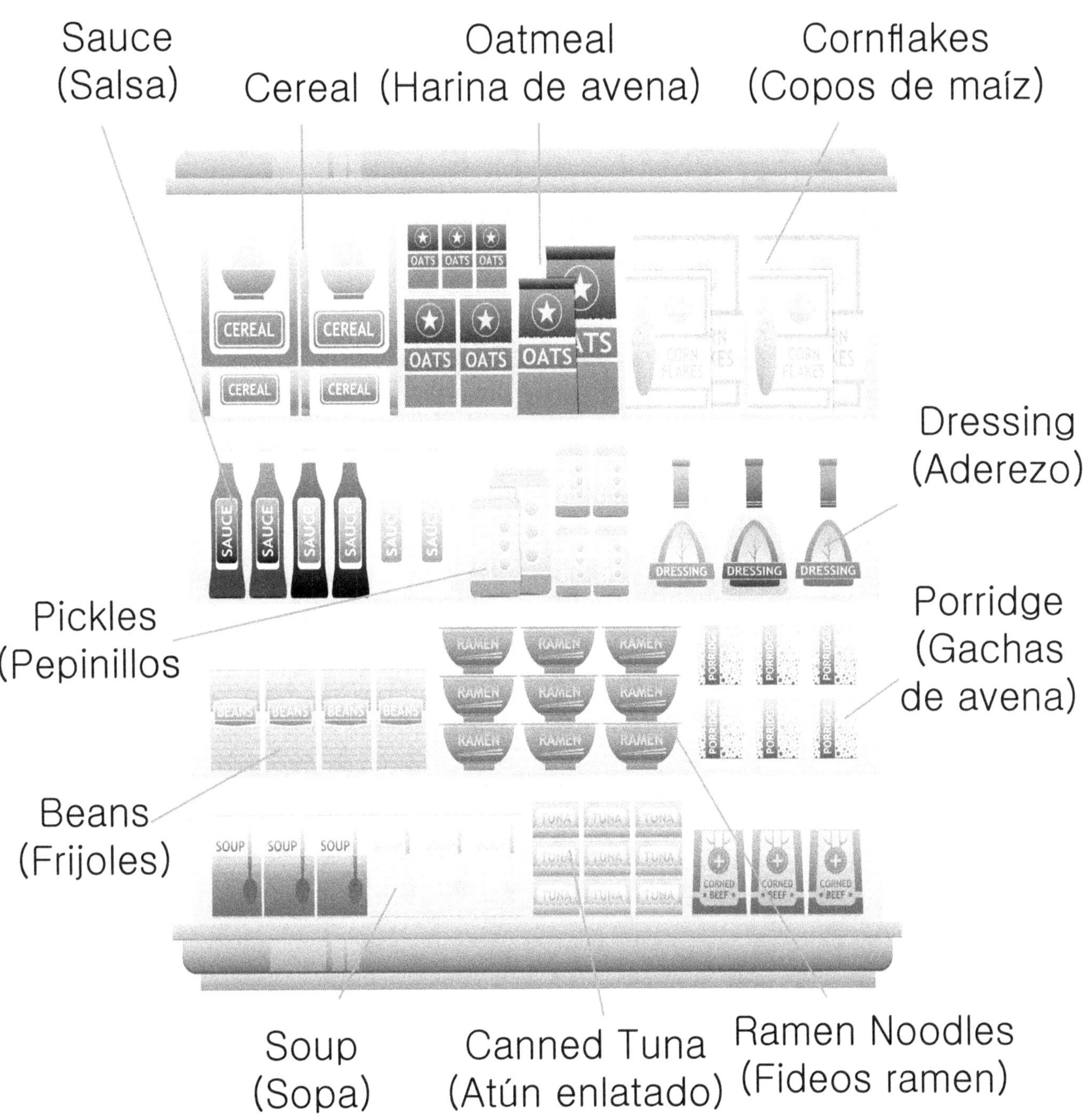

Sauce
(Salsa)
Cereal
Oatmeal
(Harina de avena)
Cornflakes
(Copos de maíz)
Dressing
(Aderezo)
Pickles
(Pepinillos
Porridge
(Gachas
de avena)
Beans
(Frijoles)
Soup
(Sopa)
Canned Tuna
(Atún enlatado)
Ramen Noodles
(Fideos ramen)
CEREAL
OATS
CORN FLAKES
SAUCE
DRESSING
BEANS
RAMEN
PORRIDGE
SOUP
TUNA
CORNED BEEF

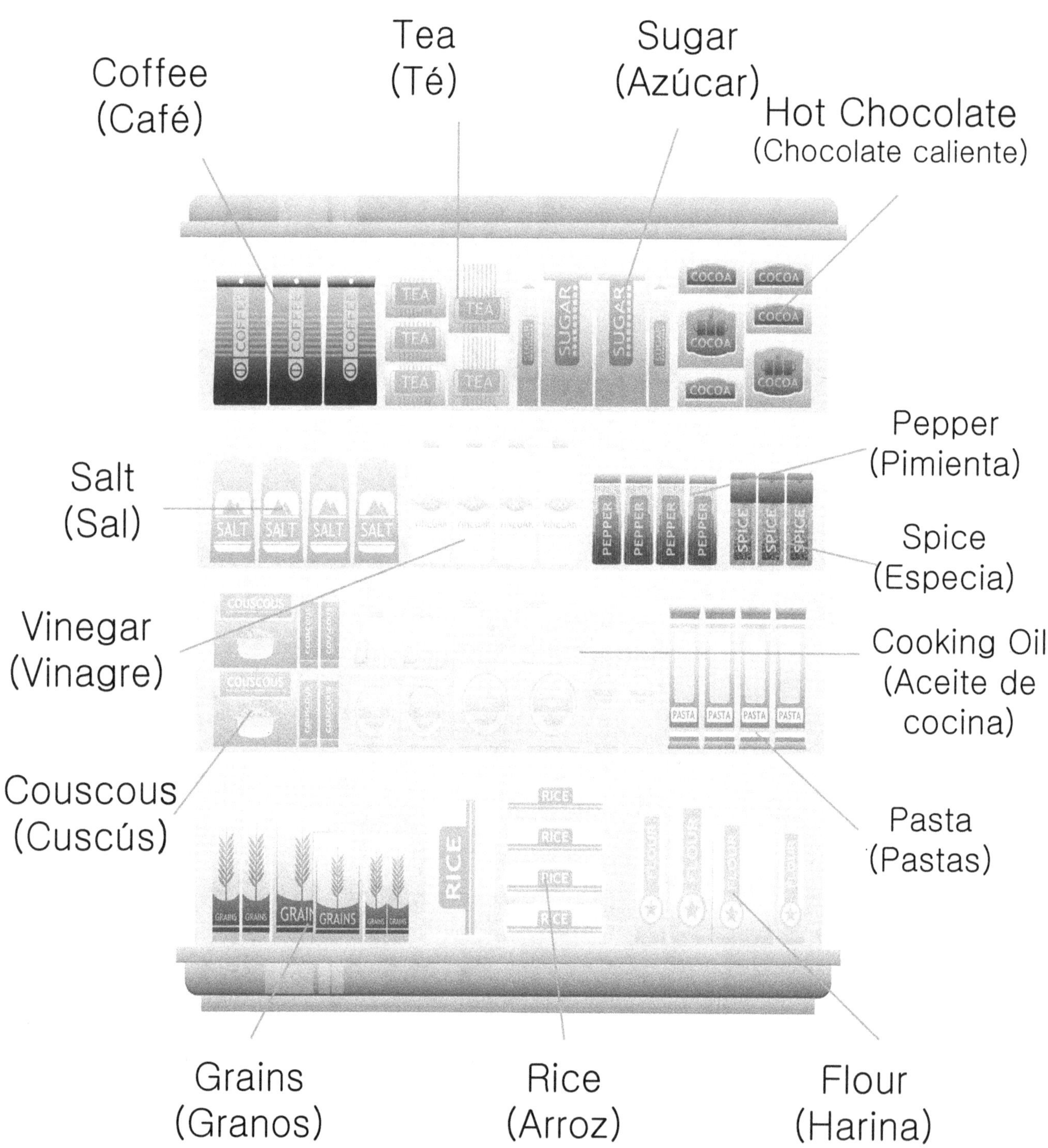

Coffee
(Café)
Tea
(Té)
Sugar
(Azúcar)
Hot Chocolate
(Chocolate caliente)
COCOA
COCOA
COCOA
COCOA
COCOA
COFFEE
TEA
SUGAR
Salt
(Sal)
SALT
Pepper
(Pimienta)
PEPPER
SPICE
Spice
(Especia)
Vinegar
(Vinagre)
COUSCOUS
Cooking Oil
(Aceite de cocina)
PASTA
Couscous
(Cuscús)
Pasta
(Pastas)
GRAINS
GRAIN
RICE
FLOUR
Grains
(Granos)
Rice
(Arroz)
Flour
(Harina)

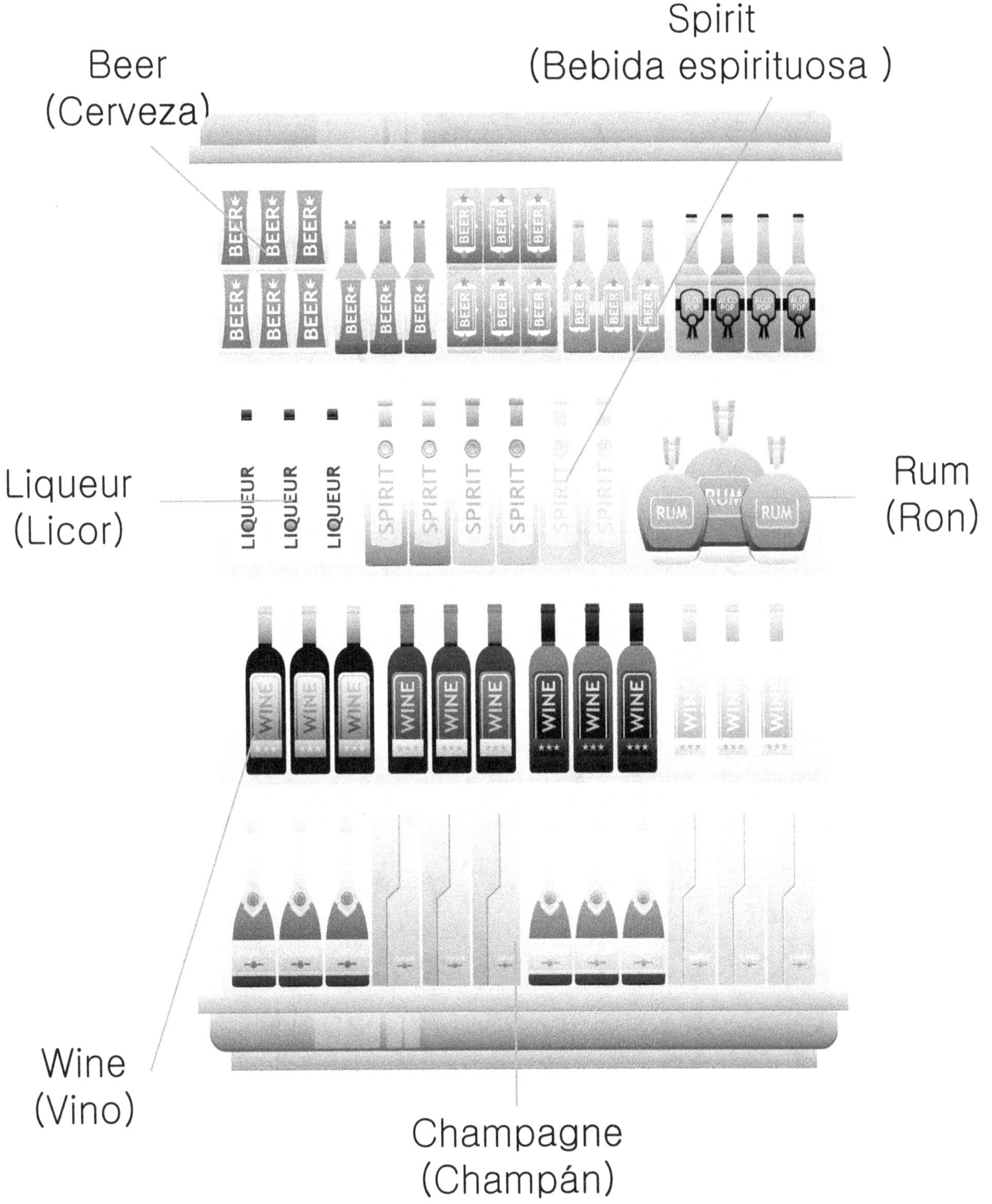
Beer
(Cerveza)
Spirit
(Bebida espirituosa)
BEER
Liqueur
(Licor)
LIQUEUR
SPIRIT
RUM
Rum
(Ron)
ALCO POP
WINE
Wine
(Vino)
Champagne
(Champán)

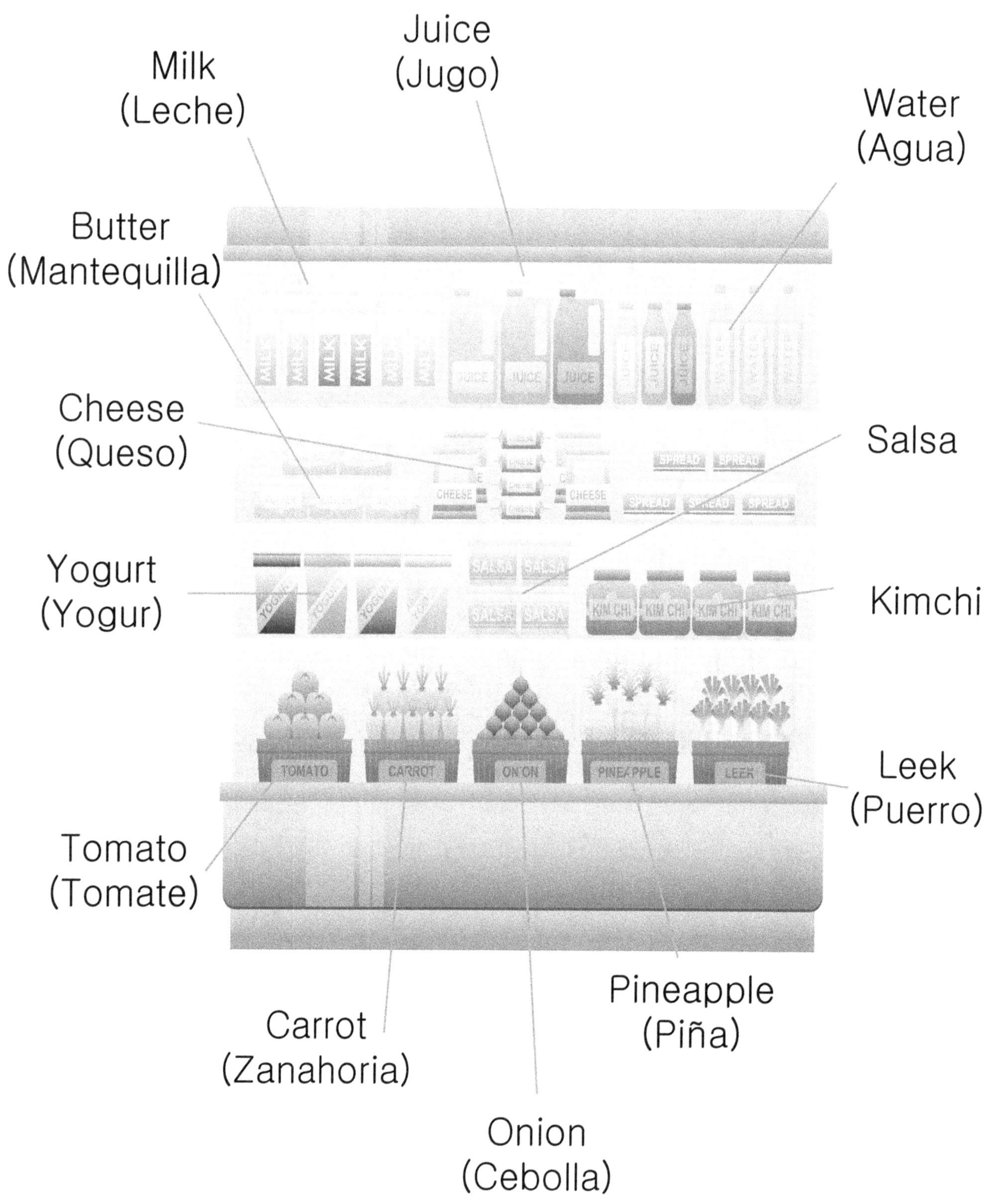

Milk
(Leche)
Juice
(Jugo)
Water
(Agua)
Butter
(Mantequilla)
Cheese
(Queso)
Salsa
Yogurt
(Yogur)
Kimchi
Tomato
(Tomate)
Leek
(Puerro)
Carrot
(Zanahoria)
Pineapple
(Piña)
Onion
(Cebolla)
MILK
JUICE
CHEESE
SPREAD
YOGUR
SALSA
KIM CHI
TOMATO
CARROT
ONION
PINEAPPLE
LEEK

GENTE (사람)

Firefighter
(Bombero)

Mailman
(Cartero)

Police Officer
(Oficial de policia)

목수 (Carpintero)

Musician (Músico)

Singer (Cantante)

Engineer (Ingeniero)

Scientist (Científico)

Doctor

Cook/Chef (Cocinero)

Hairdresser (Peluquero)

Barber (Barbero)

Teacher (Profesor)

Student (Estudiante)

Photographer
(Fotógrafo)

Fisherman
(Pescador)

Nurse (Enfermera)

Actor

Tailor (Sastre)

Farmer (Agricultor)

Plubmer (Fontanero)

Security (Guardia)

Athlete (Atleta)

Housewife (Ama de casa)

FAMILIA (가족)

Mom (Mamá)
Mother (Madre)

Dad (Papá)
Father (Padre)

Grandma (Abuela)

Grandpa (Abuelo)

Brother (Hermano)

Sister (Hermanar)

Friends (Amigos)

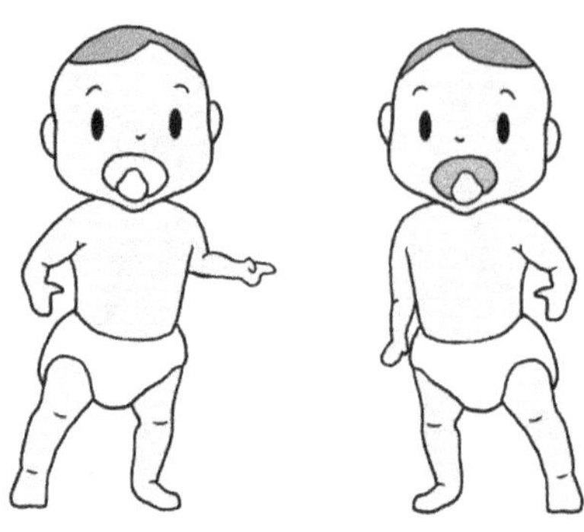

Twin (Gemelos)
Triplet (Trillizo)

Husband and Wife
(Esposo y Esposa)

Aunt (Tía)

Uncle (Tío)

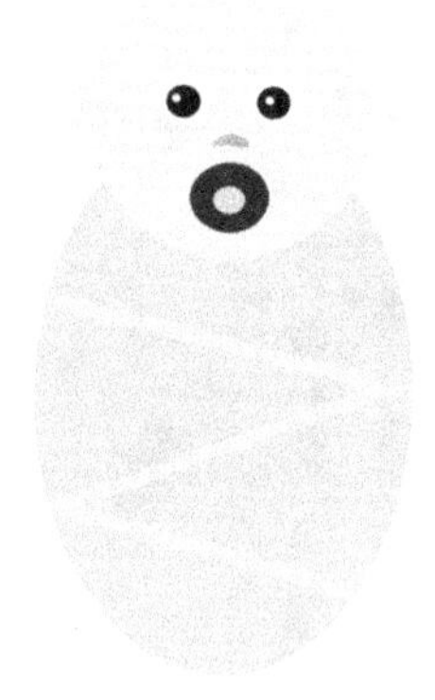

Baby (Bebé)

EMOTIONS (EMOCIONES)

In Love	Playful	Surprised	Sad
(Enamorado)	(Juguetón)	(Sorprendido)	(Triste)
Comical	Happy	Angry	Joyful
(Cómico)	(Contento)	(Enojado)	(Alegre)
Confident	Shy	Charming	Calm
(Confidente)	(Tímido)	(Encantador)	(Calma)

TRANSPORTATION (TRANSPORTE)

Navigation
(Navegación)

Air Vent
(Salida de aire)

Dashboard
(Tablero de instrumentos)

Emergency Light
(Luz de emergencia)

Rearview Mirror
(Espejo retrovisor)

Side Mirror
(Espejo lateral)

Airbag
(Bolsas de aire)

Gearbox
(Caja de cambios)

Horn
(Bocina)

Steering Wheel
(Volante)

Passenger Seat
(Asiento del pasajero)

Turn Signal
(Señal de vuelta)

Wheel
(Rueda)
Widnshield
(Parabrisas)
Door Handle
(Manija de la puerta)
Roof
(Techo)
Trunk
(El maletero)
Bumper
(Parachoque)
Tail Light
(Luz de la cola)
License Plate
(Placa)
Headlight
(Faro)
Tire
(Neumático)
Fog Light
(Luz de niebla)
Door
(Puerta)
Hood
(Capó del coche)

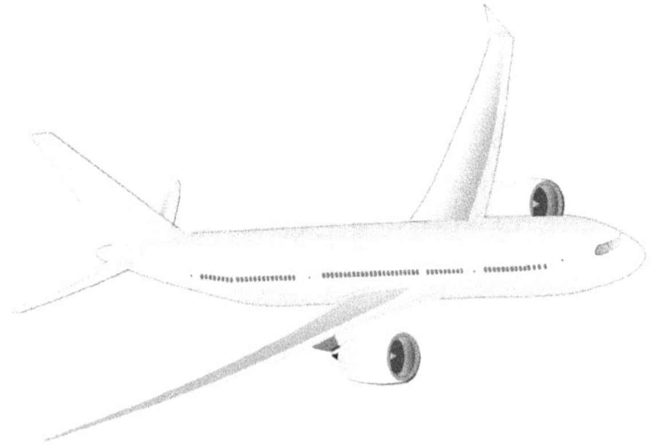

Airplane (Avión)

Bus (Autobús)

Bicycle (Bicicleta)

Motorcycle (Motocicleta)

Train (Tren)

Subway (Subterraneo)

Helicopter
(Helicóptero)

Express Bus
(Autobús exprés)

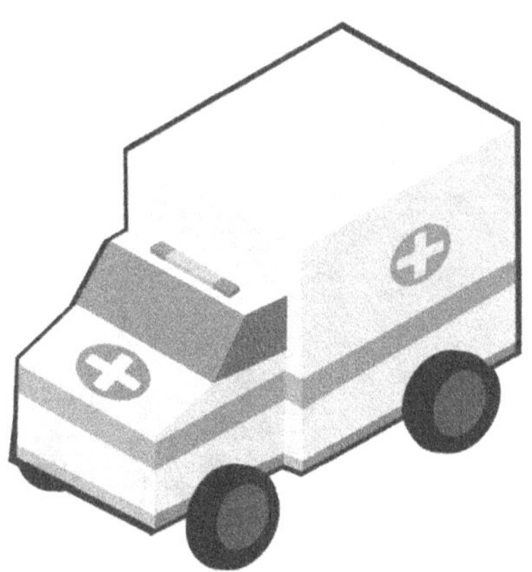

Ambulance
(Ambulancia)

Ship (Enviar)

Taxi

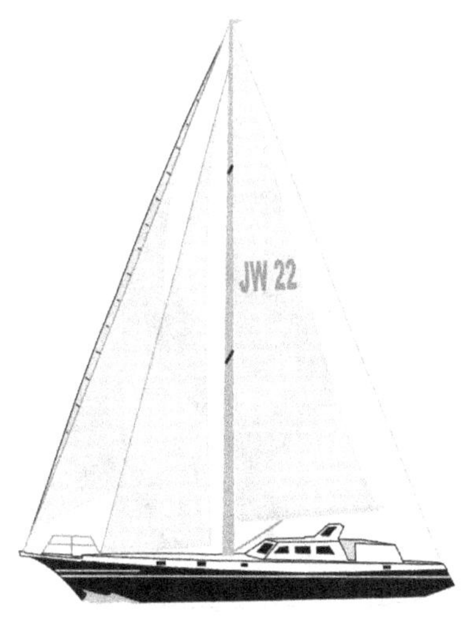

Yacht (Yate)

Captain (Capitán)

Pilot (Piloto)

운전사 (Conductor)

Train Engineer
(Ingeniero de tren)

Sailor (Marinero)

Flight Attendent
(Auxiliar de vuelo)

Passenger (Pasajero)

In-flight Meal
(Comida en vuelo)

Life Vest (Chalecos salvavidas)

Emergency Exit
(Salida de emergencia)

Stairs (Escalera)

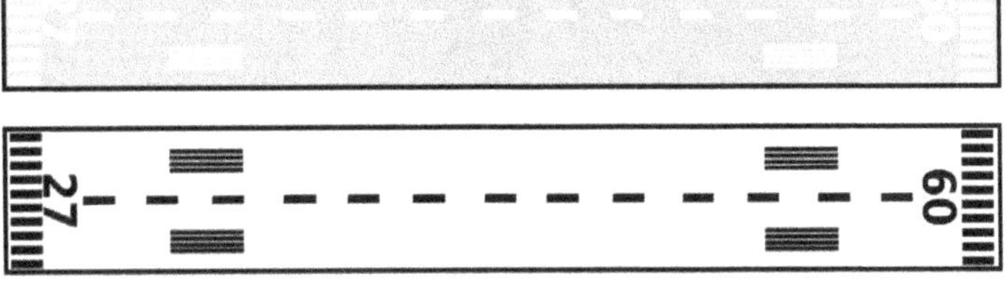

Runway (Pista)

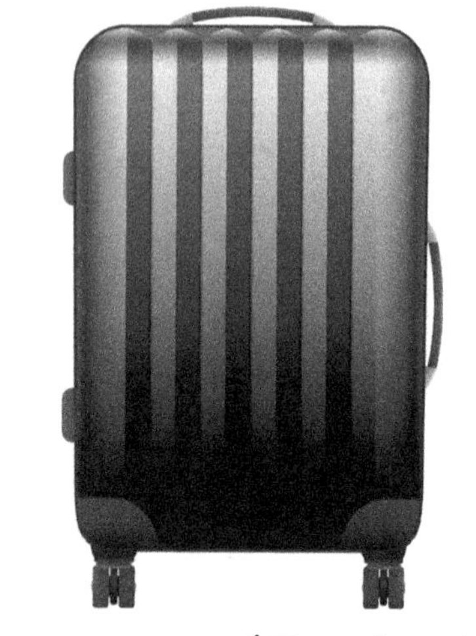

Luggage (Equipaje)

Lock (Candado)

Security Guard
(Personal de mantemieno)

Boarding Pass
(Tarjeta de embarque)

Passport (Pasaporte)

Identification Card
(Tarjeta de identificación)

SPORTS (DEPORTES)

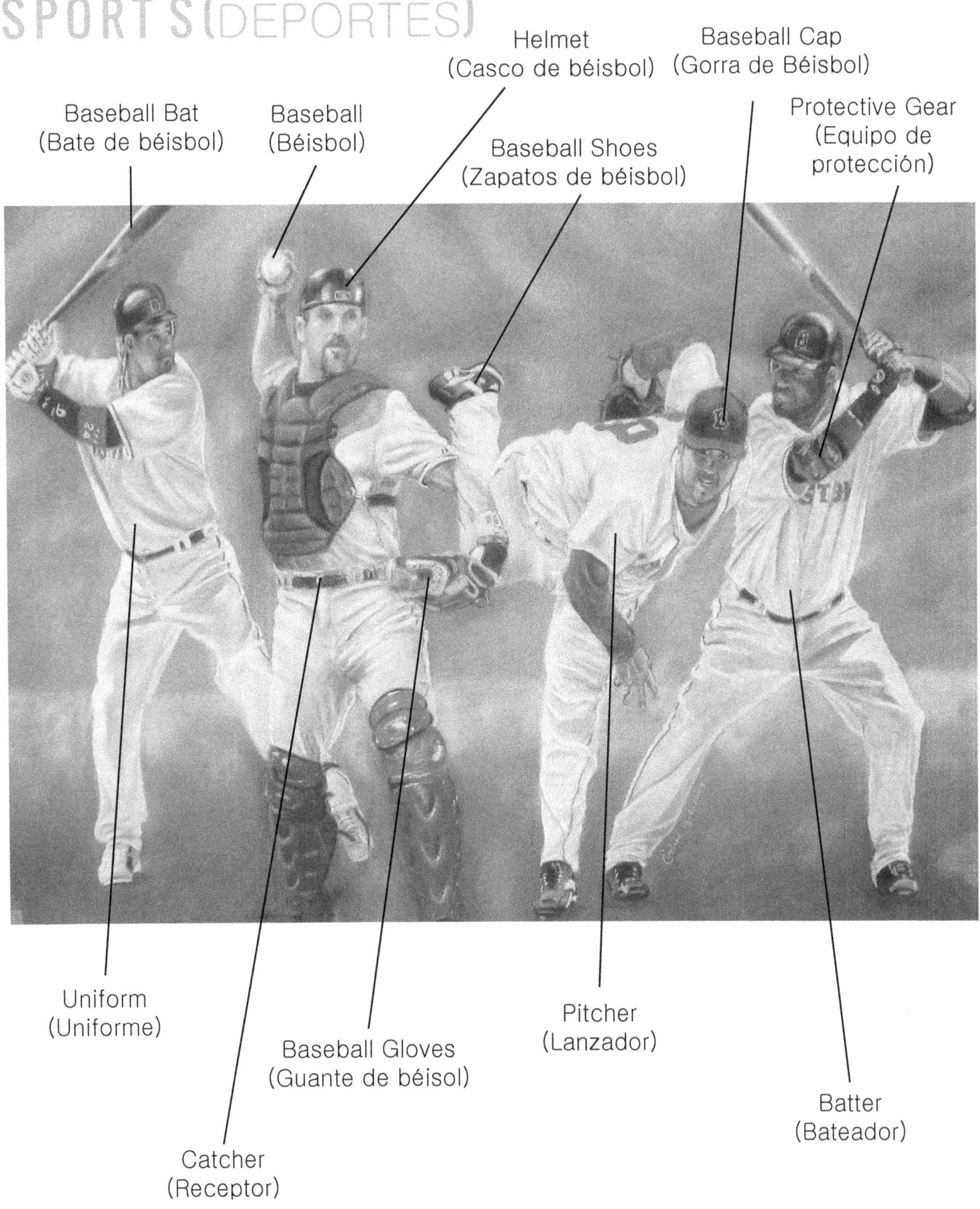

Baseball (Béisbol)

Soccer (Fútbol)

Volleyball
(Voleibol)

American Football
(Fútbol Americano)

Ice Hockey
(Hockey sobre hielo)

Basketball
(Baloncesto)

Running (Carrera)

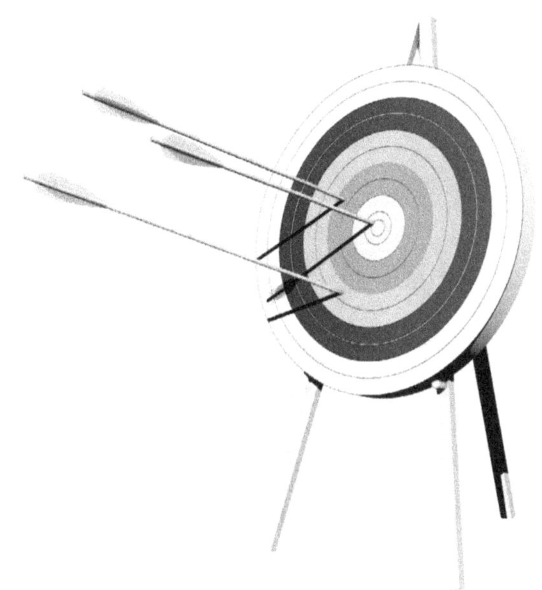

Archery
(Tiro al arco)

Boxing (Boxeo)

Horse Racing
(Las carreras de caballos)

Table Tennis
(Tenis de mesa)

Tae Kwon Do

Referee (Árbitro)

Stadium (Estadio)

Admission Ticket
(Boleto de admisión)

Audience
(Audiencia)

Podium (Podios)

Finish Line (Línea de meta)

Baseball Bat
(Bate de béisbol)

Soccer Shoes
(Zapatos de Fútbol)

Trophy (Trofeo)

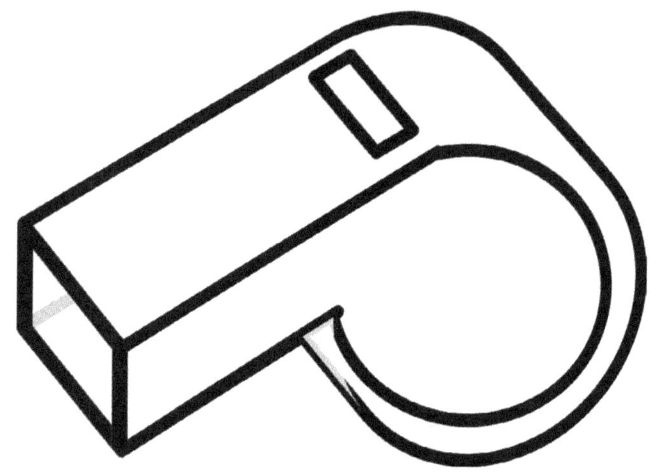

Whistle (Silbato)

Jersey (Traje deportivo)

Baseball Glove
(guante de béisbol)

Jump Rope
(Cuerda de salto)

Chin Up (Barra fija)

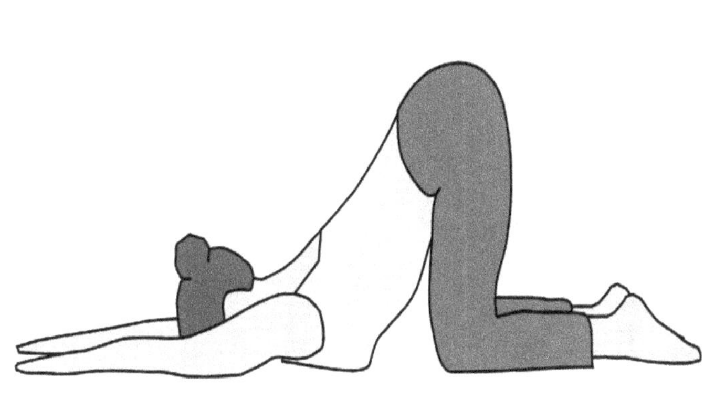

Yoga

Sit-up
(Ejercicio abdominal)

Treadmill (Rueda de andar)

ANIMALS (ANIMALES)

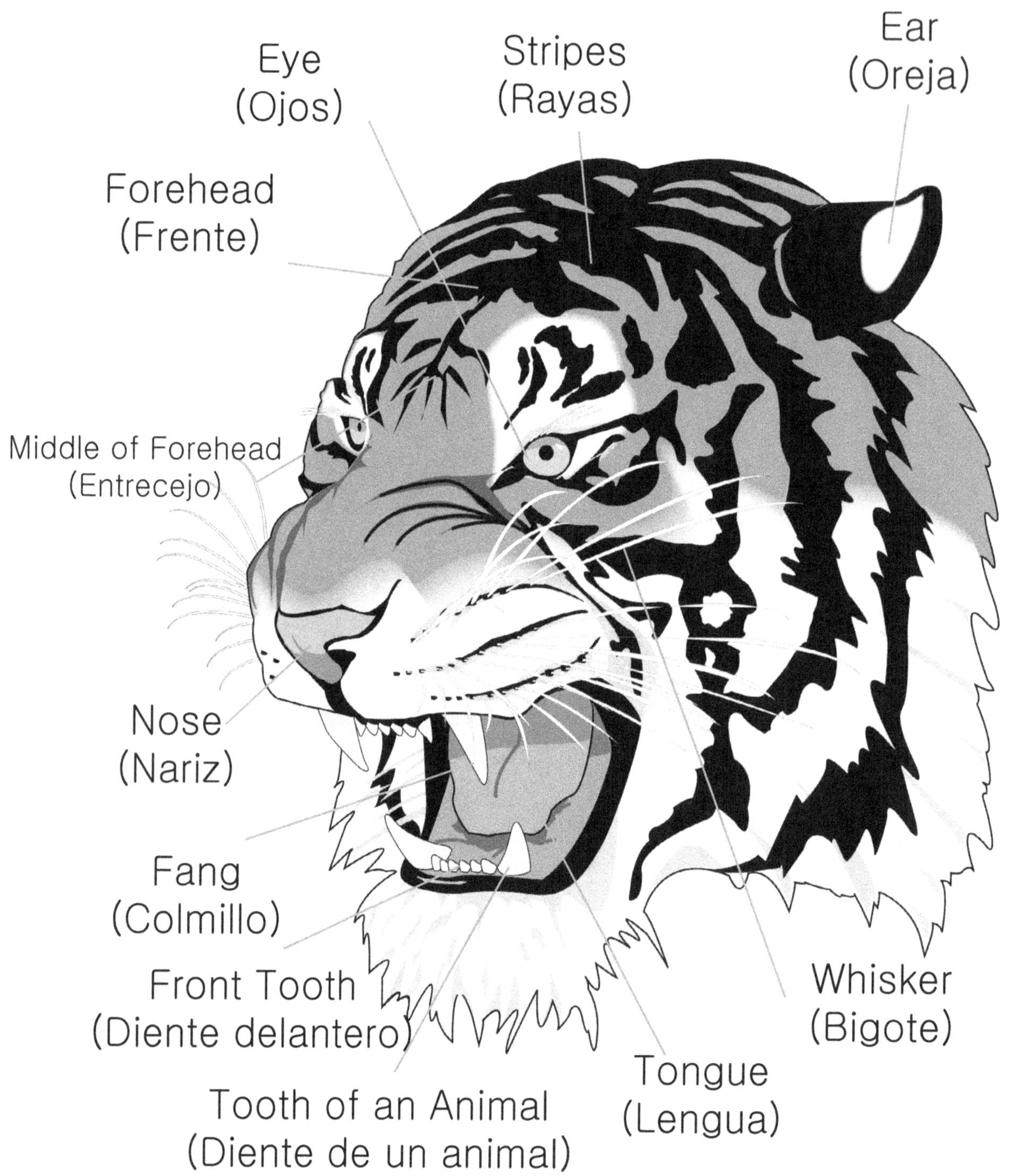

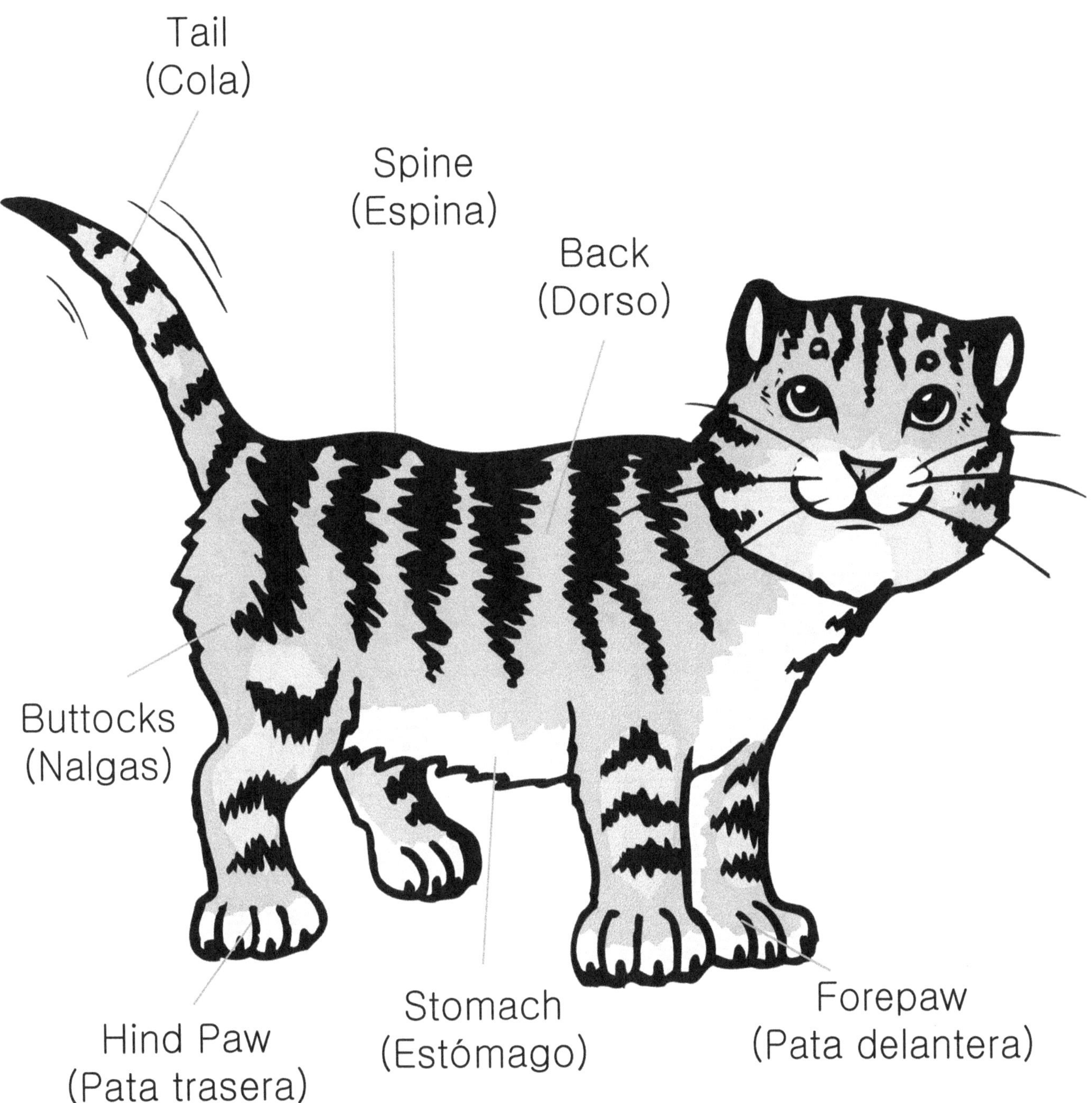
Tail
(Cola)
Spine
(Espina)
Back
(Dorso)
Buttocks
(Nalgas)
Hind Paw
(Pata trasera)
Stomach
(Estómago)
Forepaw
(Pata delantera)

Elephant (Elefante)

Lion (León)

Rhinoceros
(Rinoceronte)

Giraffe (Jirafa)

Cow (Vaca)

Sloth (Perezoso)

Sheep (Oveja)

Horse (Caballo)

Dog (Perro)
Puppy (Perrito)

Cat (Gato)
Kitten (Gatito)

Hippo (Hipopótamo)

Rabbit (Conejo)

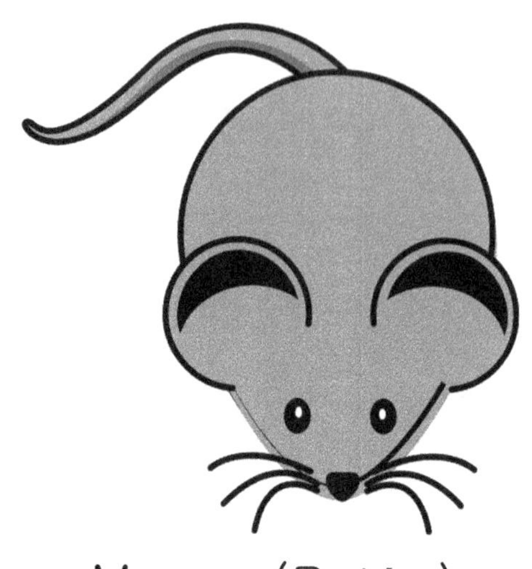

Antelope (Antílope)

Mouse (Ratón)

Tiger (Tigre)

Wolf (Lobo)

Deer (Ciervo)

Monkey (Mono)

Leopard (Leopardo)

Zebra (Cebra)

Fox (Zorro)

Hedgehog (Erizo)

Mole (Topo)

Squirrel (Ardilla)

Badger (Tejón)

Raccoon (Mapache)

Dolphin (Delfín)

Otter (Nutria)

Seal (Foca)

Bear (Oso)

BIRDS (AVES)

Wing
(Ala)

Feather
(Pluma)

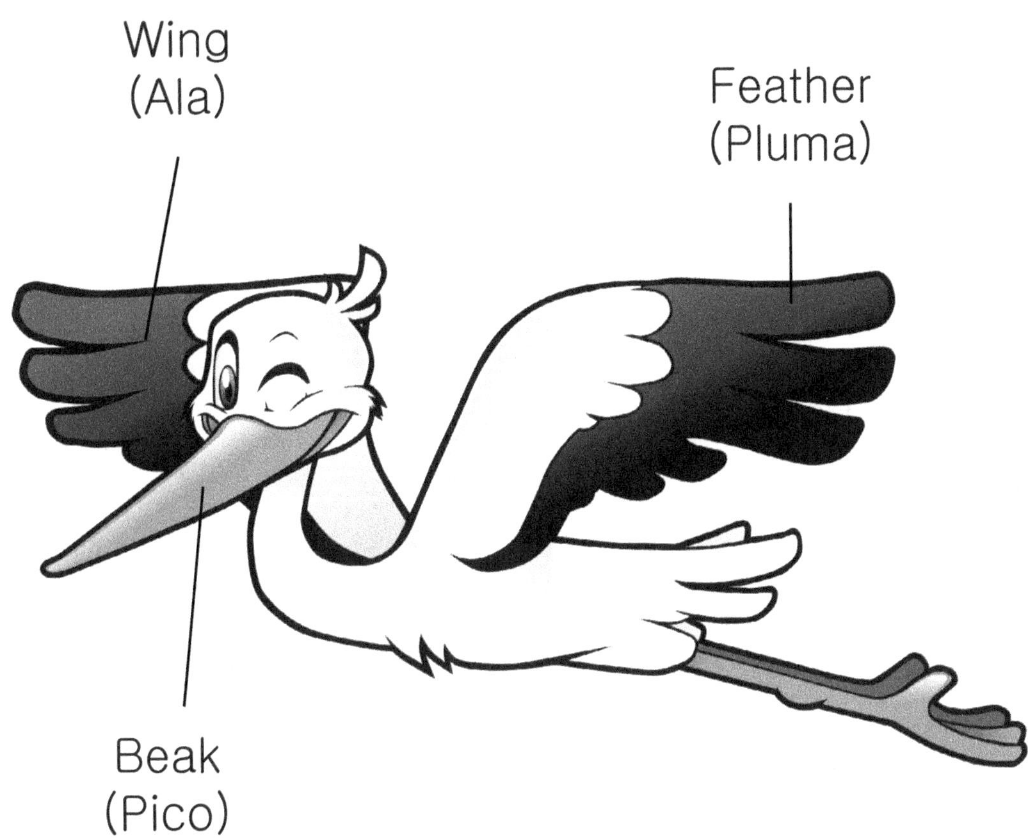

Beak
(Pico)

Chicken (Pollo)

Duck (Pato)

Goose (Ganso)

Eagle (Águila)

Parrot (Loro)

Owl (Búho)

Crane (Grua)

Swan (Cisne)

Gull (Gaviota)

Ostrich (Avestruz)

Penguin (Pingüino)

Crow (Cuervo)

Peacock (Pavo real)

Turkey (Guajolote)

Bluebird
(Azulejo pajaro)

Sparrow (Gorrión)

Hawk (Halcón)

Stork (Cigüeña)

INSECTS (INSECTOS)

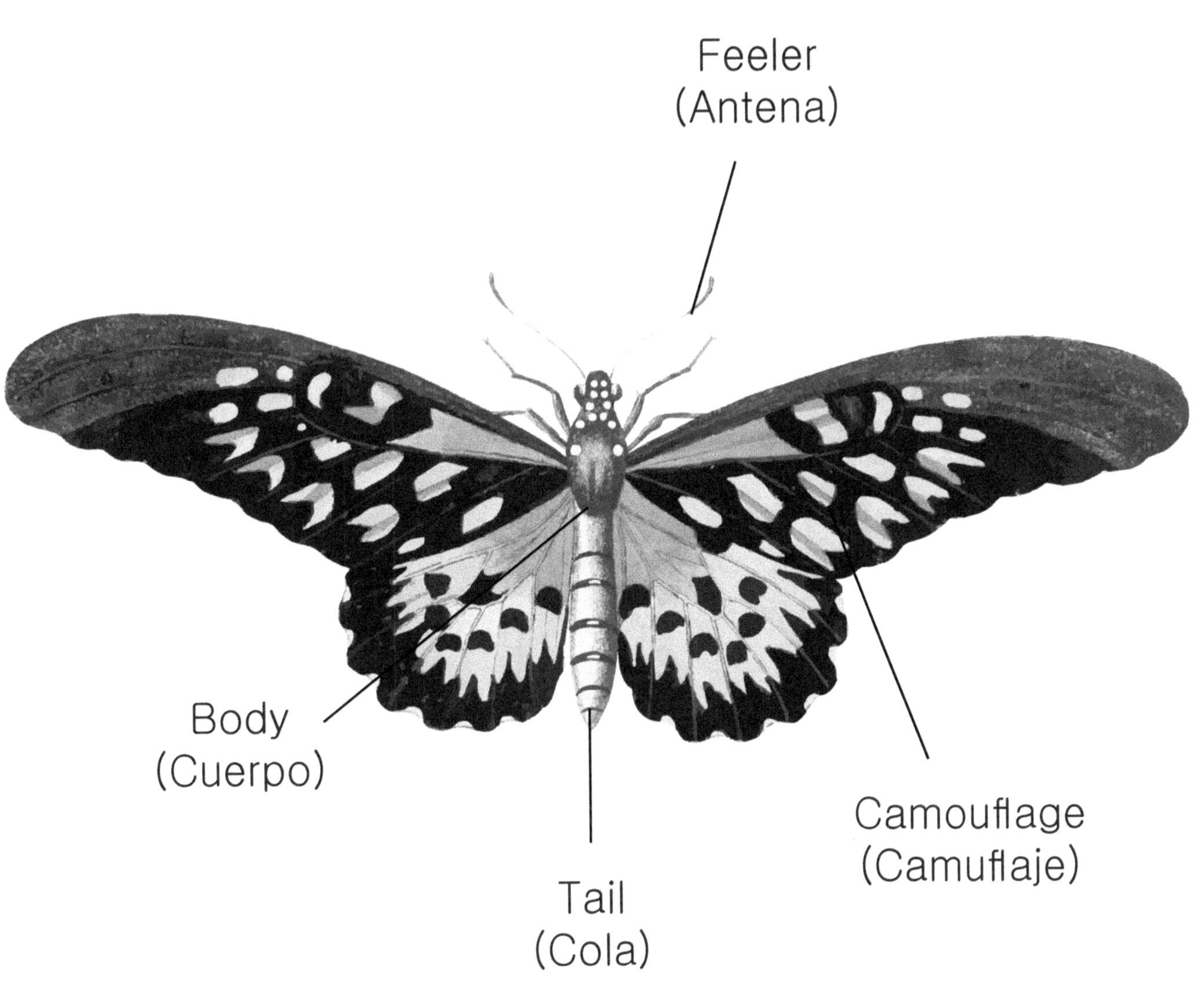

Butterfly
(Mariposa)

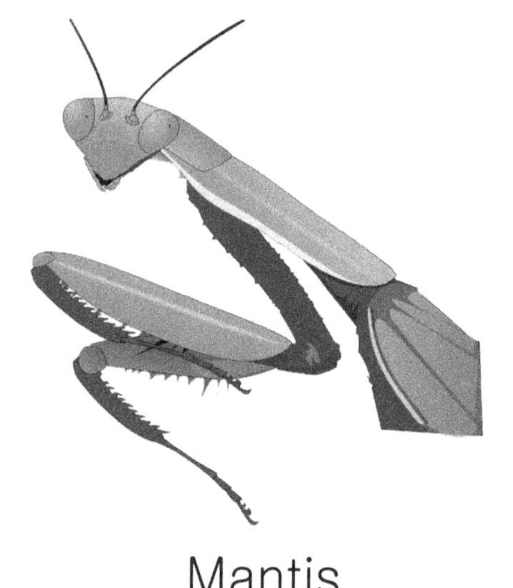

Mantis

Ant (Hormiga)

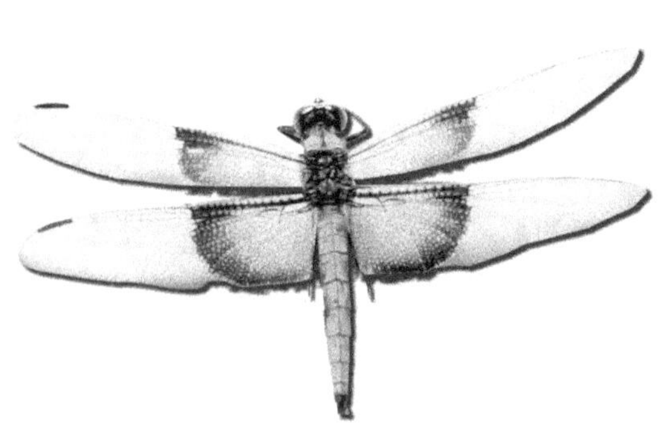
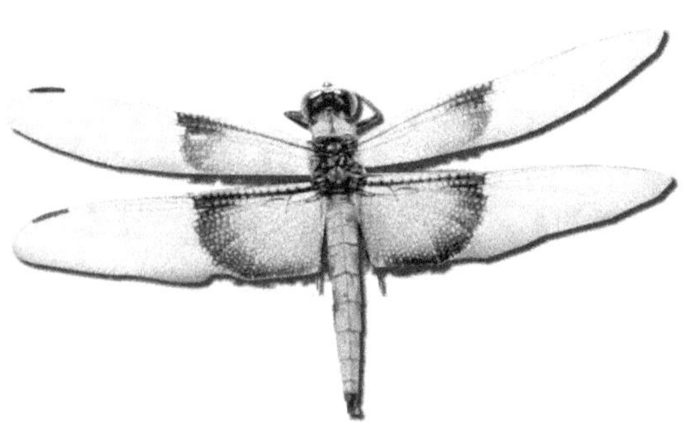

Dragonfly
(Libélula)

Moth (Polilla)

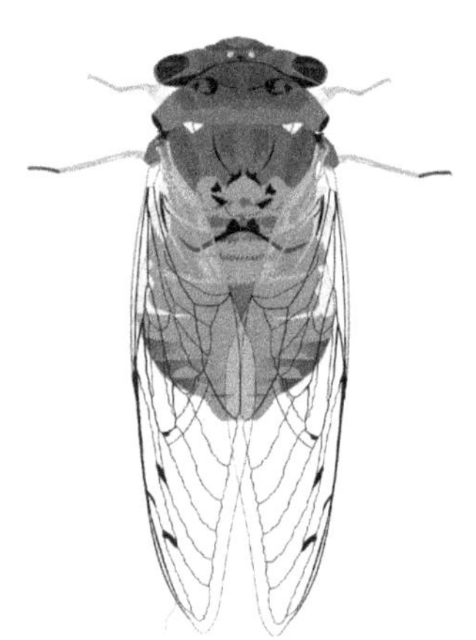

Cicada (Cigarra)

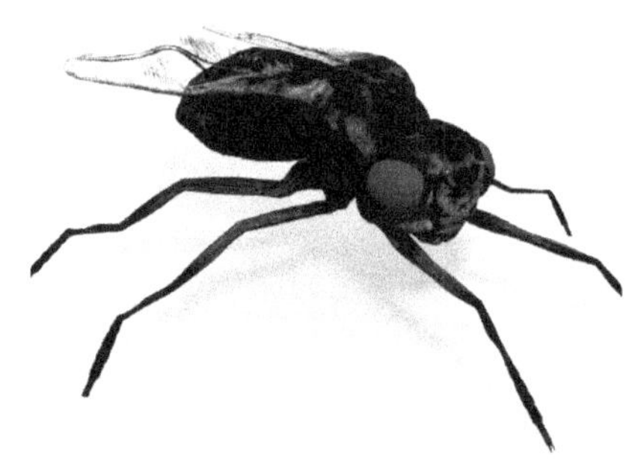

Fly (Mosca)

Mosquito

Ladybug (Mariquita)

Bee (Abeja)

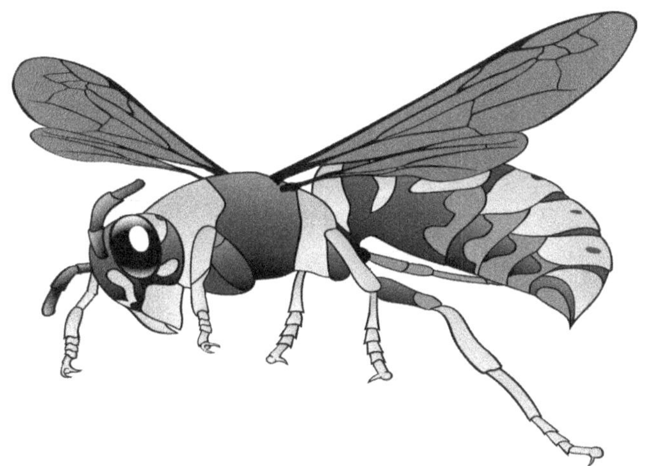

Wasp (Avispa)

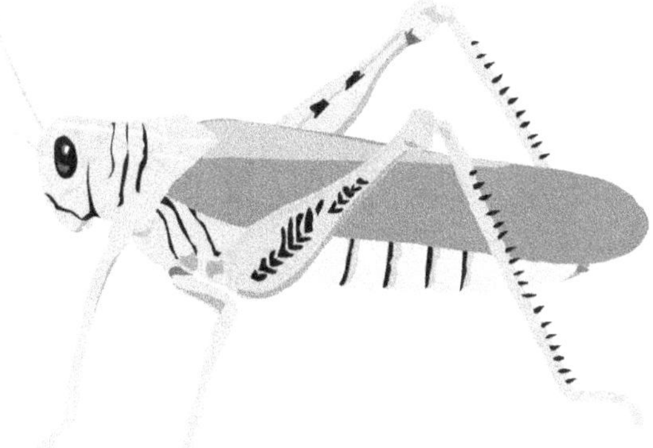

Grasshopper
(Saltamontes)

Larva

Centipede (Ciempiés)

Cricket (Grillo)

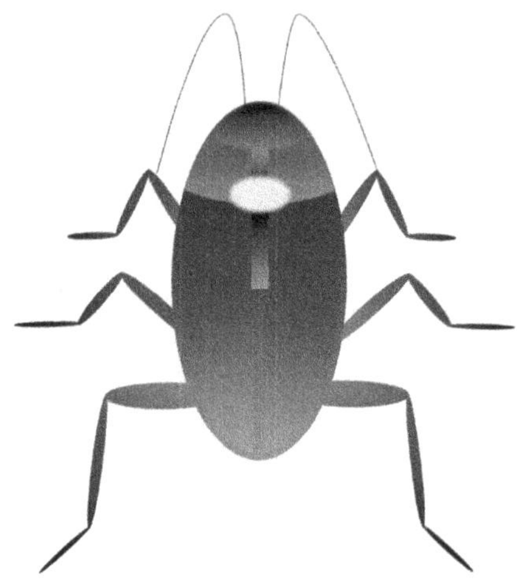

Roach
(Cucaracha)

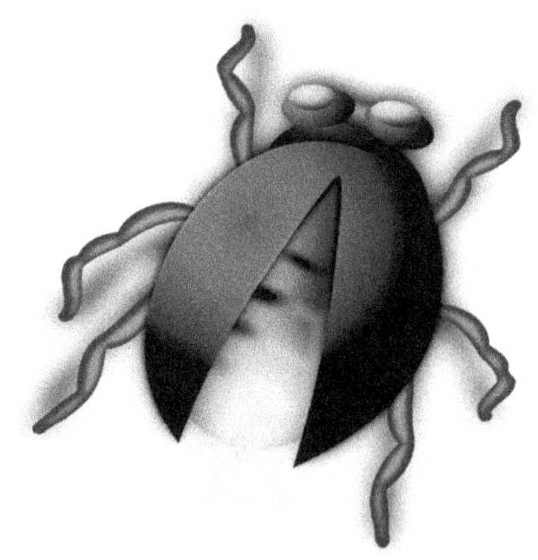

Firefly
(Luciérnaga)

Beetle (Escarabajo)

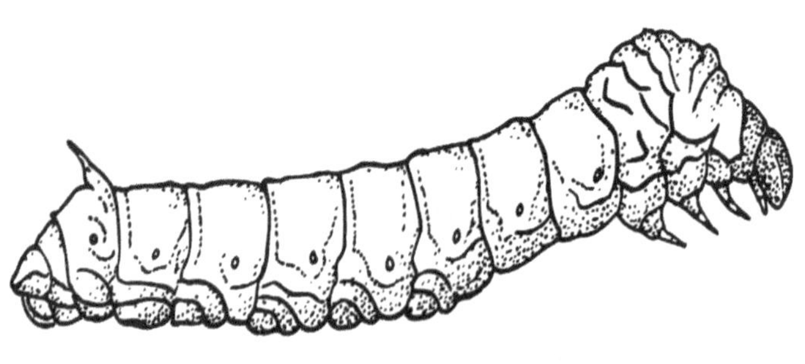

Silkworm (Gusano de seda)

FISH/MARINE LIFE (PESCADO/VIDA MARINA)

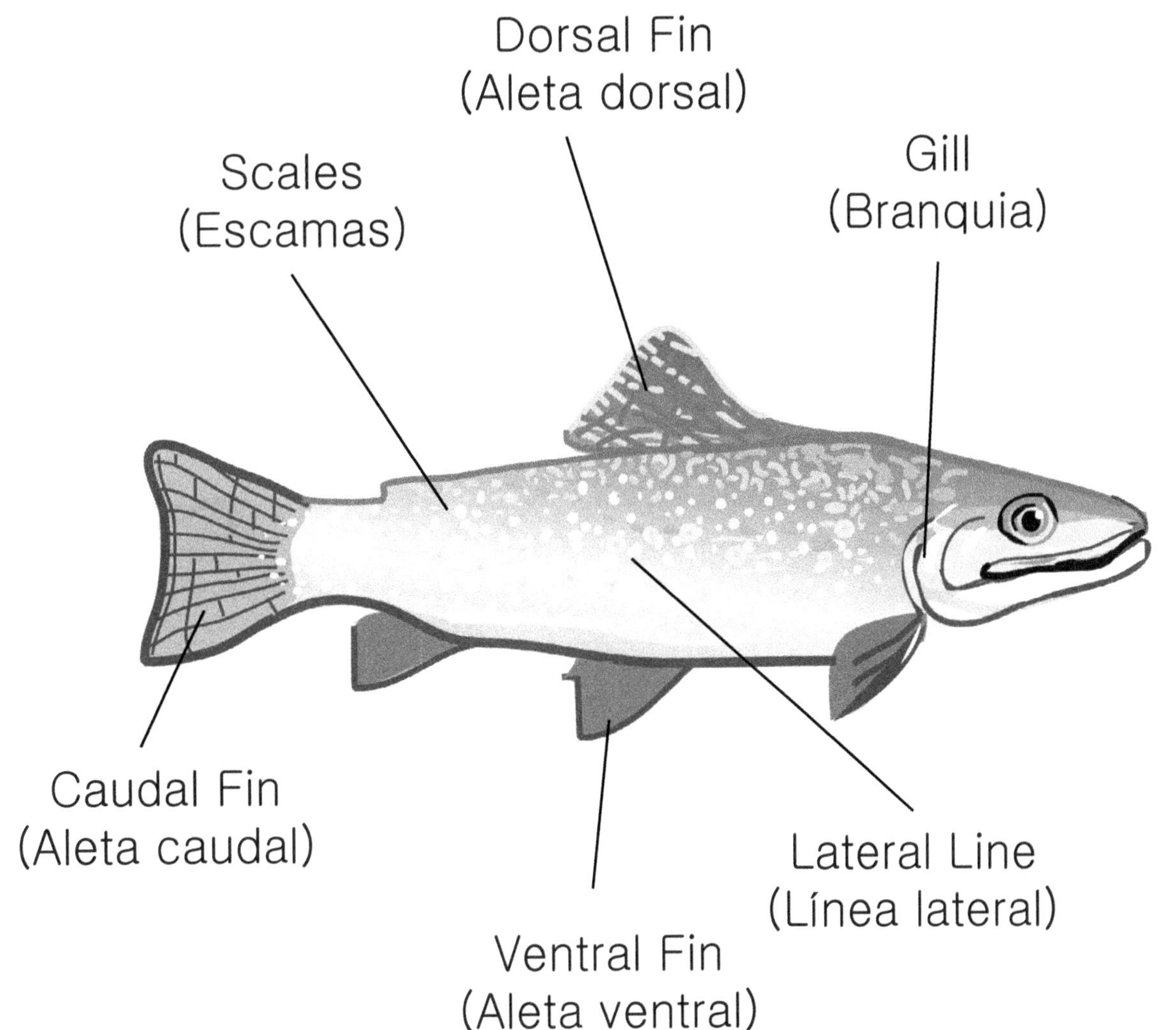

Shark (Tiburón)

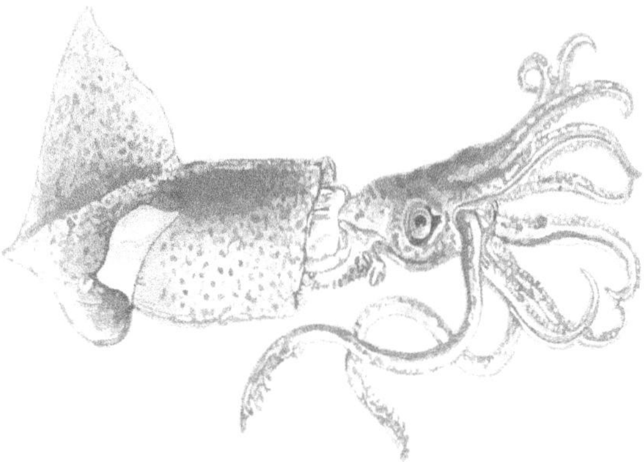

Squid (Calamar)

Octopus (Pulpo)

Carp (Carpa)

Starfish (Estrella de mar)

Jellyfish (Medusa)

Seahorse
(Caballo de mar)

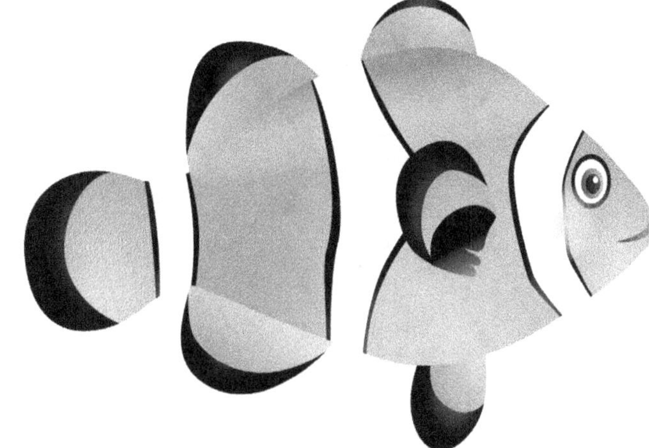

Tropical Fish
(Pez tropical)

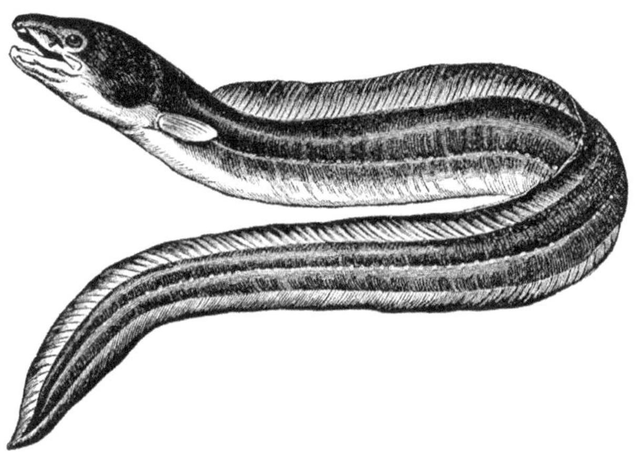

Eel (Anguila)

Tuna (Atún)

Turtle (Tortuga)

Conch (Concha)

Crawfish
(Cangrejo de río)

Shrimp (Camarón)

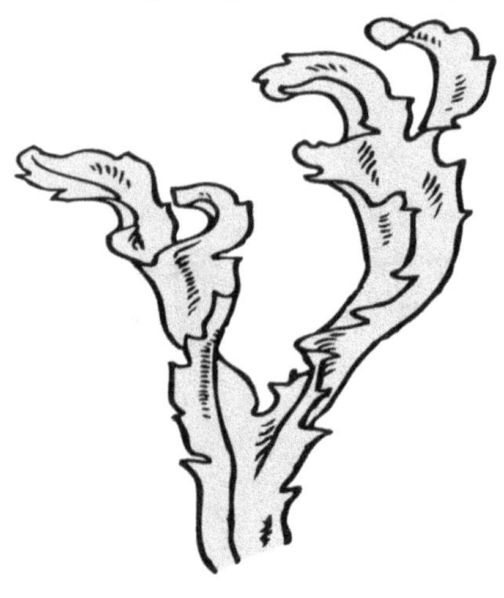

Seaweed
(Algas marinas)

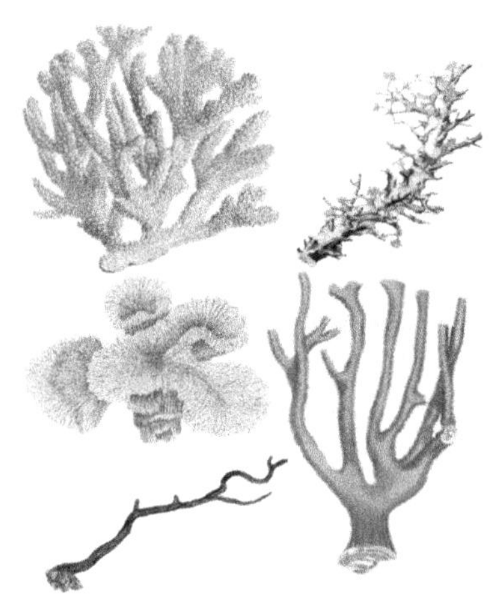

Coral

Swordfish (Pez espada)

Oyster (Ostra)

REPTILES/AMPHIBIANS (REPTILES/ANFIBIOS)

Lizard (Lagartija)

Snake (Serpiente)

Alligator (Caimán)

Chameleon
(Camaleón)

Toad (Sapo)

Frog (Rana)

Iguana

Dinosaur (Dinosaurio)

Rattlesnake
(Serpiente de cascabel)

Salamender (Salamandra)

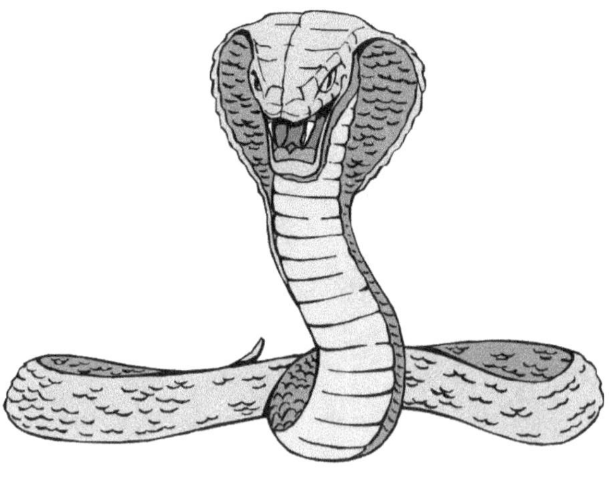

Cobra

PLANTS/FRUITS/NUTS/VEGETABLES
(PLANTAS/FRUTAS/UNECES/VERDURAS)

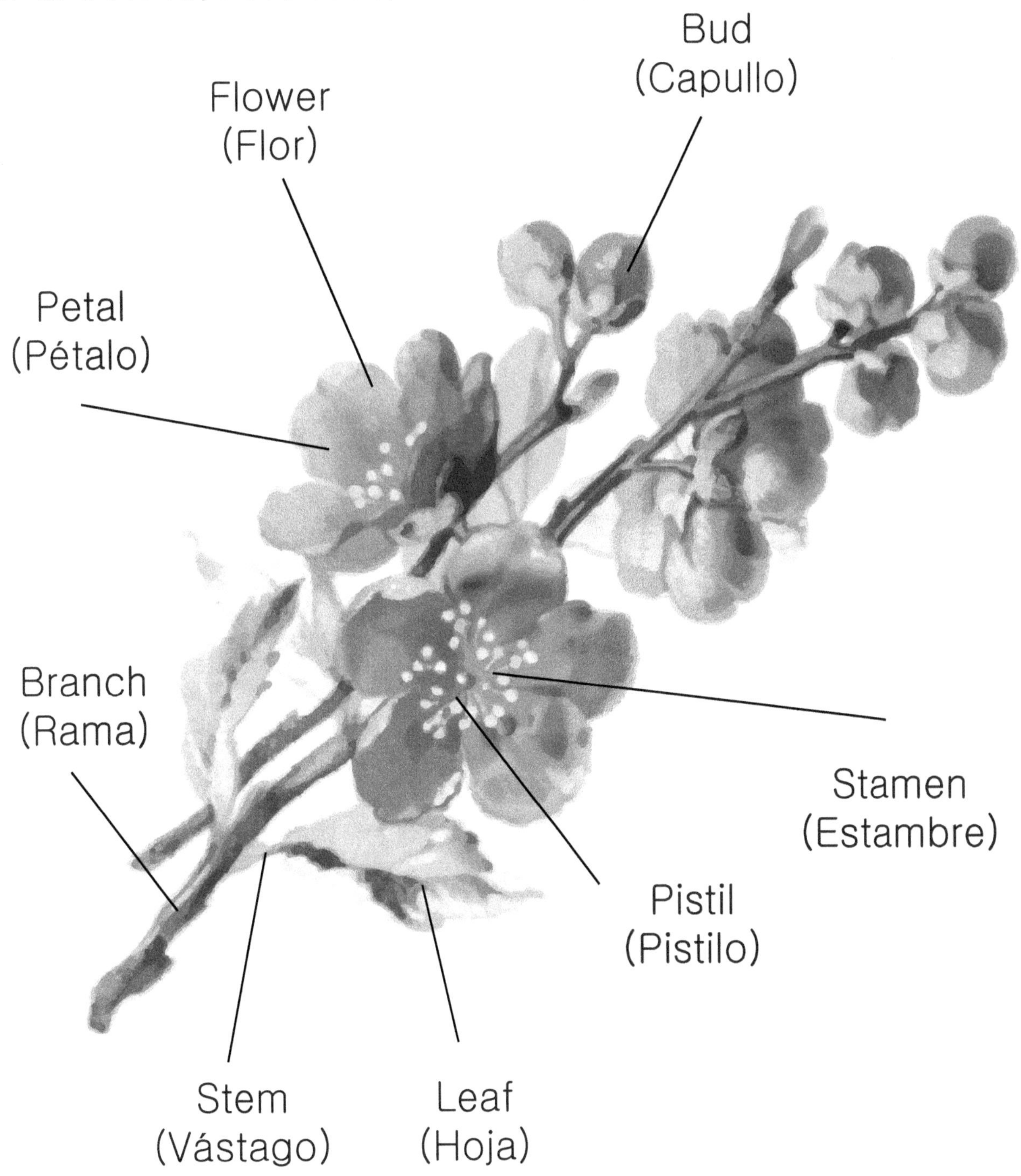

Rose (Rosa)

Sunflower (Girasol)

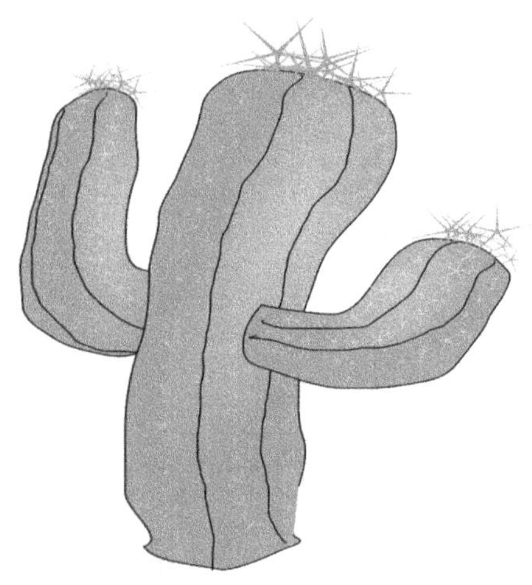

Cactus

Cherry Blossom
(Flor de cerezo)

Lotus (Loto)

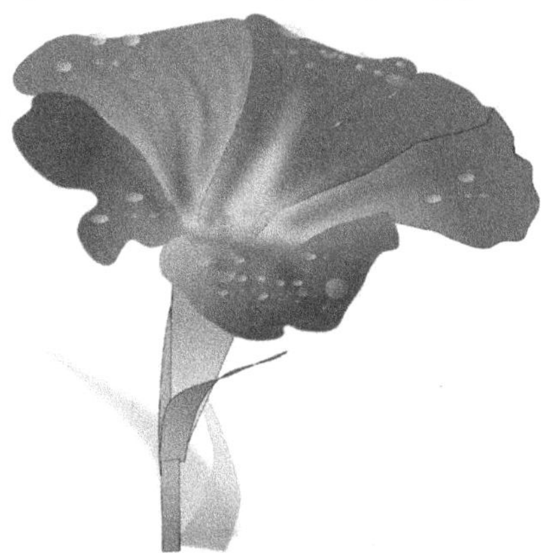

Morning Glory
(Gloria de la mañana)

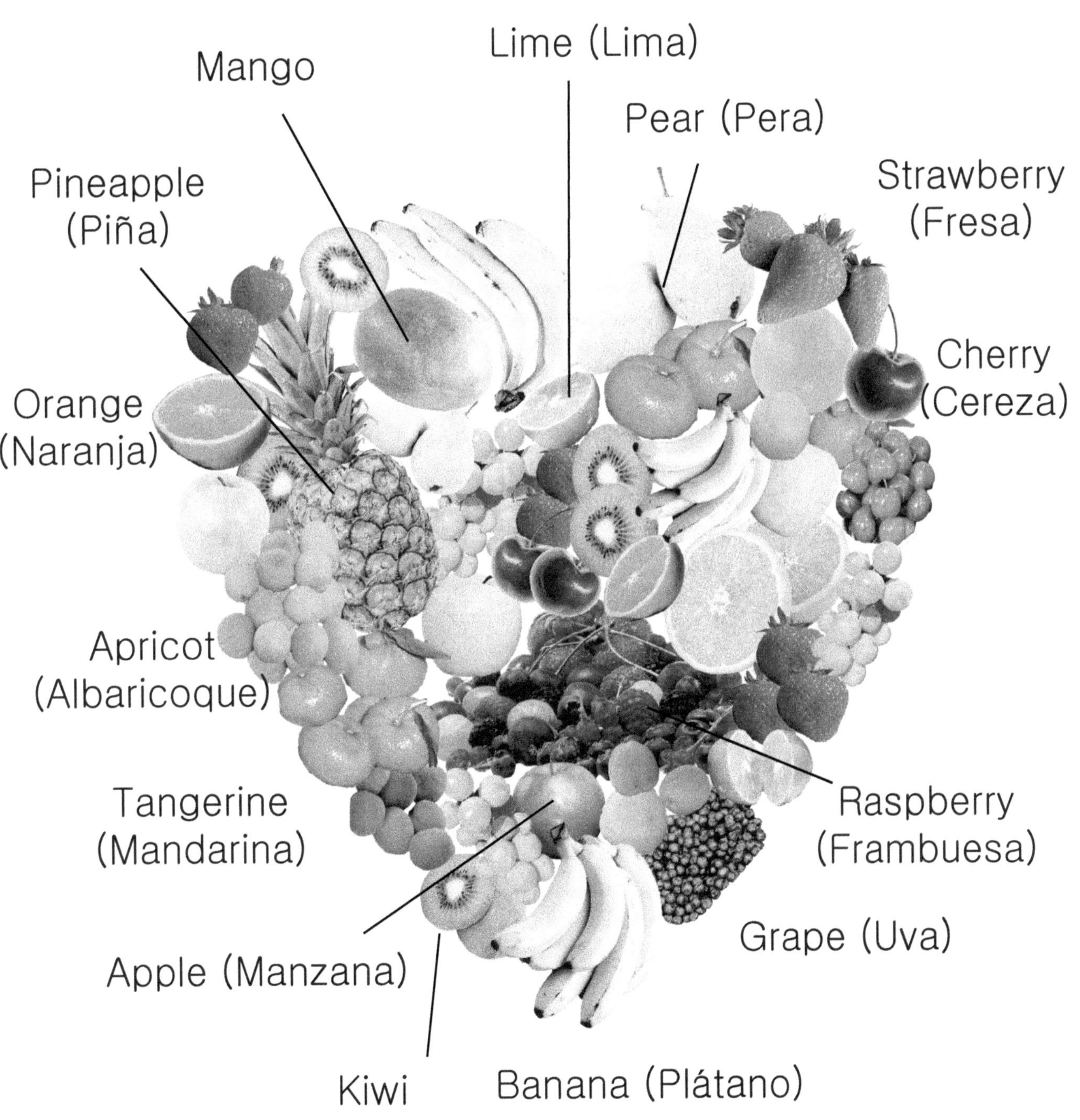

Mango
Lime (Lima)
Pear (Pera)
Pineapple (Piña)
Strawberry (Fresa)
Orange (Naranja)
Cherry (Cereza)
Apricot (Albaricoque)
Tangerine (Mandarina)
Raspberry (Frambuesa)
Apple (Manzana)
Grape (Uva)
Kiwi
Banana (Plátano)

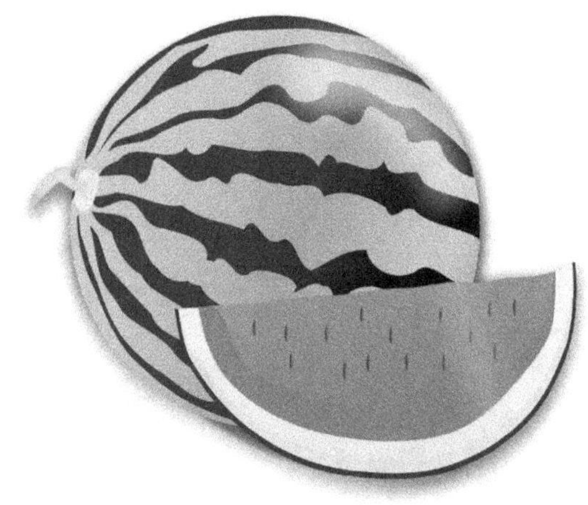

Watermelon (Sandía)

Peach (Melocotón)

Pomegranate
(Granada)

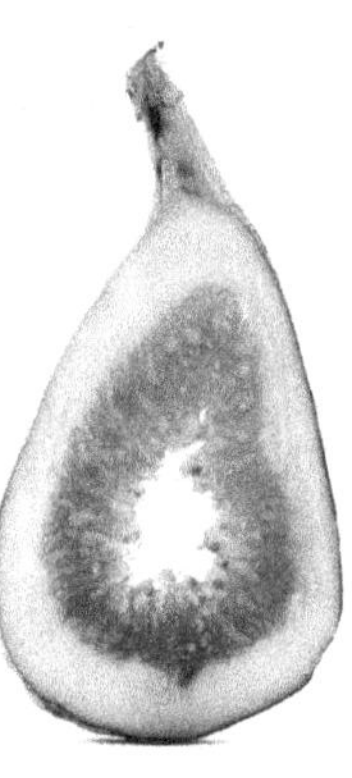

Fig (Higo)

Raisin (Pasa)

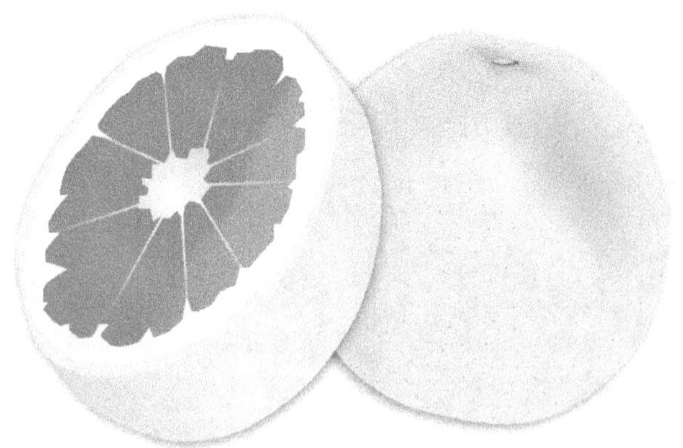

Grapefruit (Pomelo)

Walnut (Nuez)

Peanut (Maní)

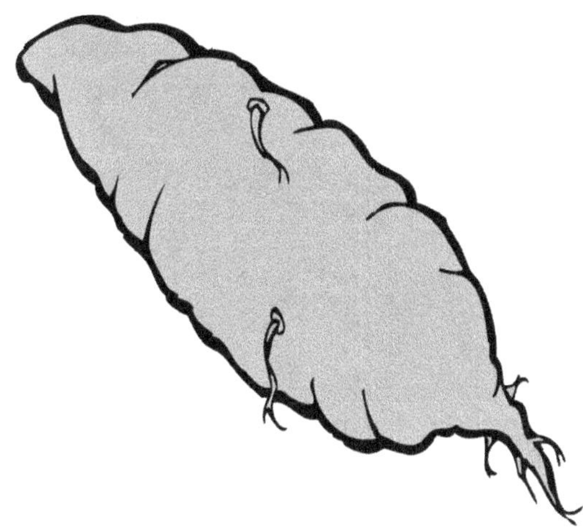

Sweet Potato
(Batata)

Chestnut (Castaña)

Onion (Cebolla)

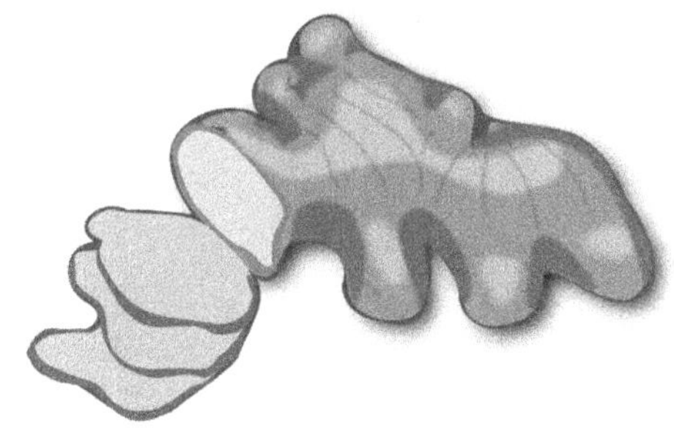

Ginger (Jengibre)

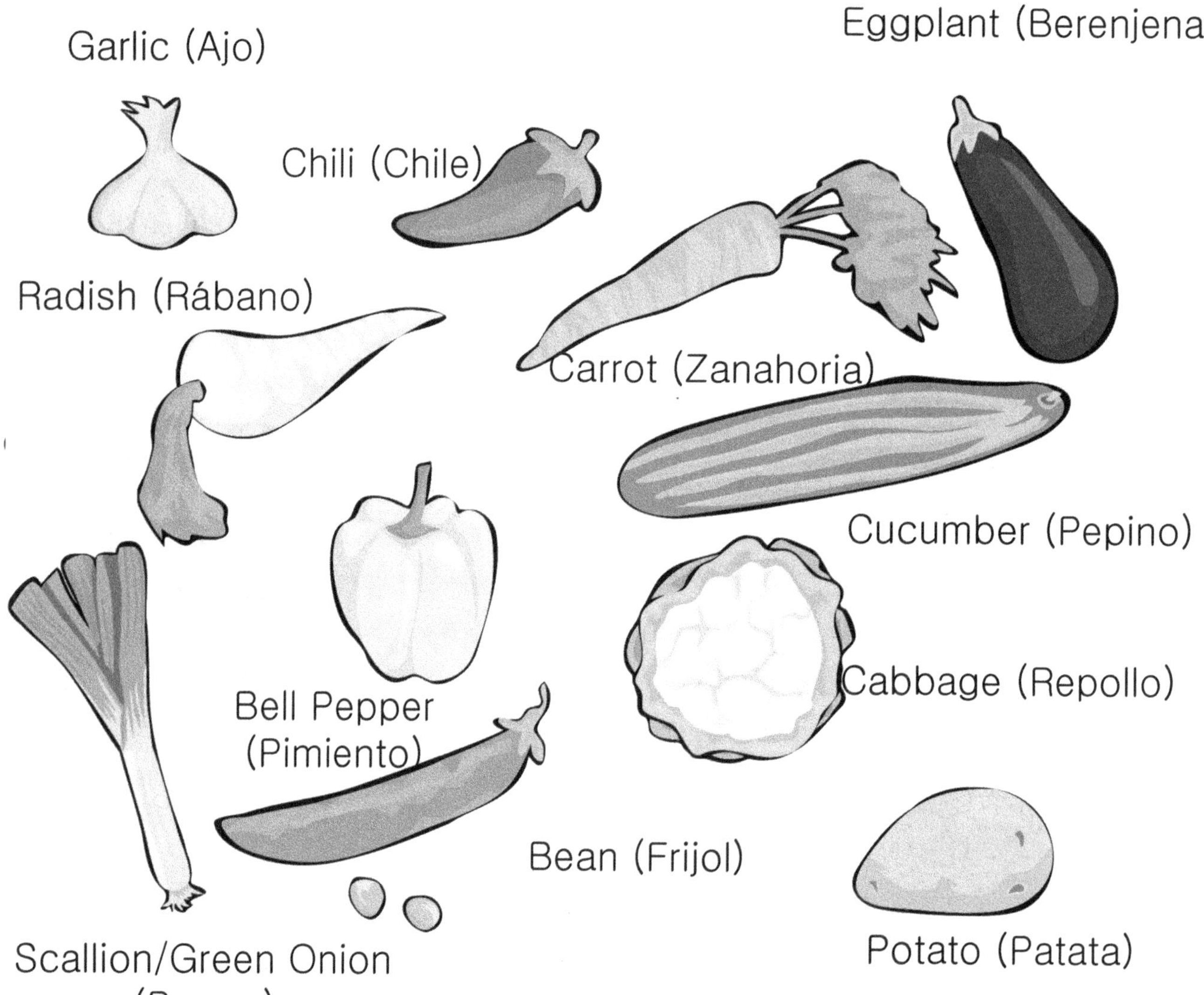

Garlic (Ajo)
Chili (Chile)
Eggplant (Berenjena)
Radish (Rábano)
Carrot (Zanahoria)
Cucumber (Pepino)
Bell Pepper (Pimiento)
Cabbage (Repollo)
Bean (Frijol)
Scallion/Green Onion (Puerro)
Potato (Patata)

SCHOOL (COLEGIO)

Classroom (Aula)

Teacher (Profesor)

Student (Estudiante)

Blackboard (Pizarra)

Desk (Escritorio)

Pencil (Lápiz)

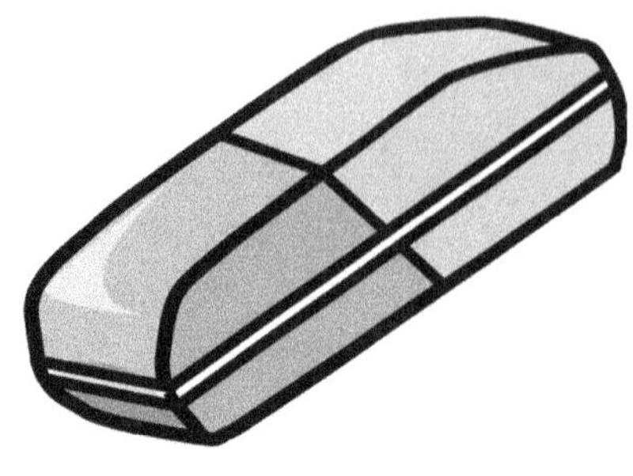

Eraser (Borrador)

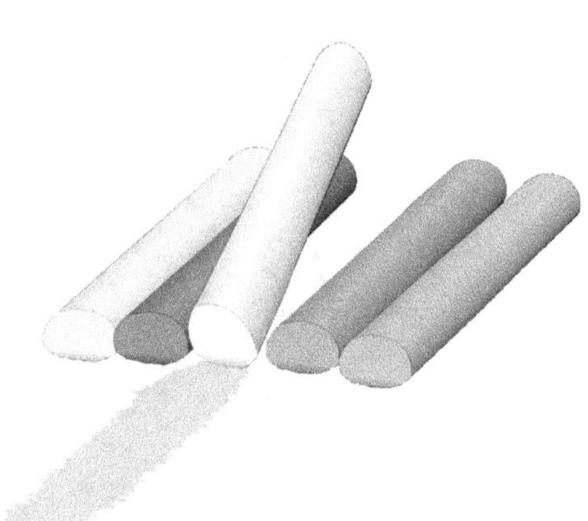

Chalk (Tiza)

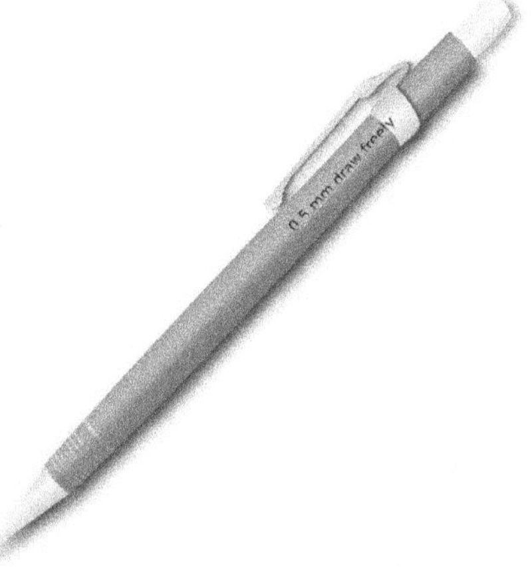

Mechanical Pencil
(Portaminas)

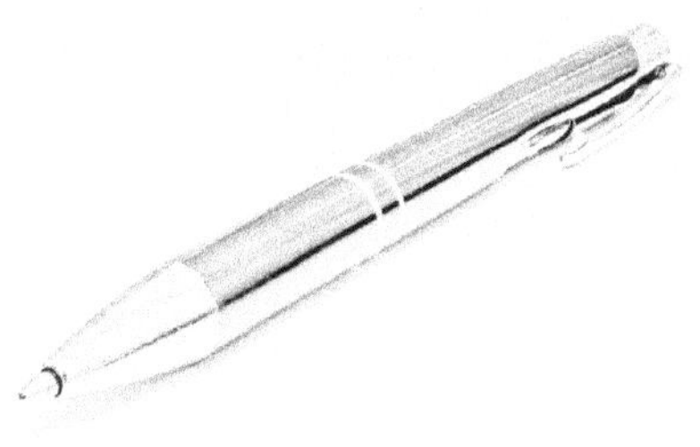

Ball-point Pen (Bolígrafo)

Notebook (Cuaderno)

Book (Libro)

Backpack (Mochila)

Box Lunch
(Portacomidas)

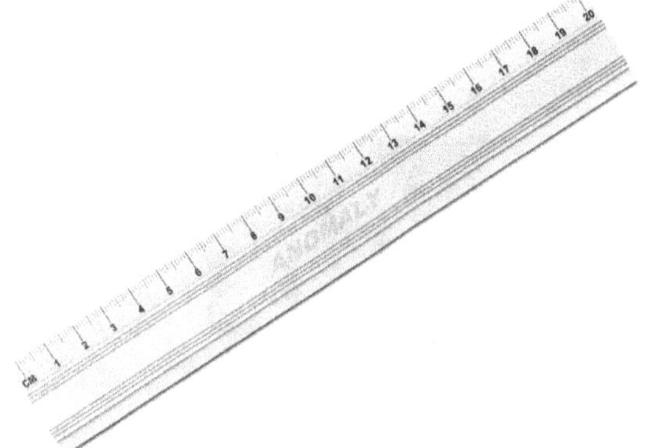

Ruler (Regla)

Gym (Gimnasio)

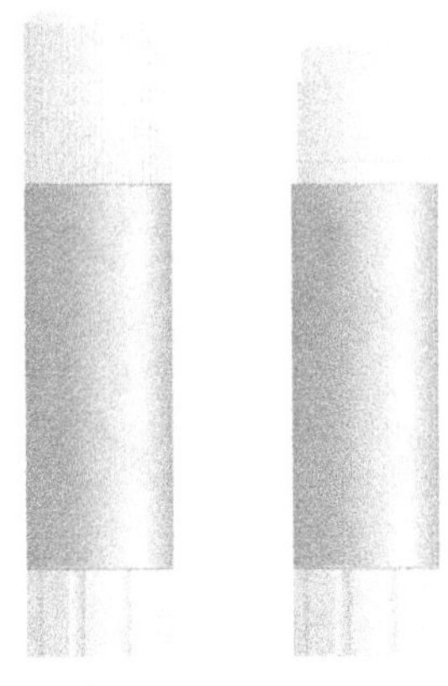

Glue (Pegamento)

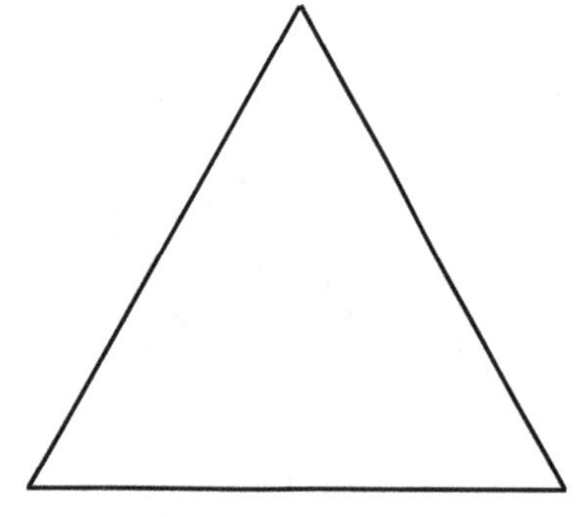

Triangle (Triángulo)

Rectangle (Rectángulo)

Square (Cuadrado)

Pentagon (Pentágono)

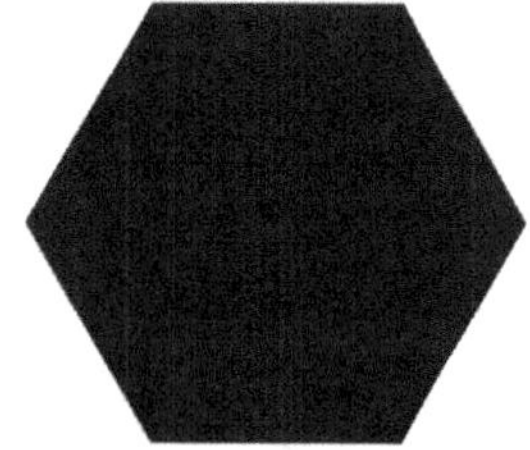

Hexagon (Hexágono)

Circle (Circulo)

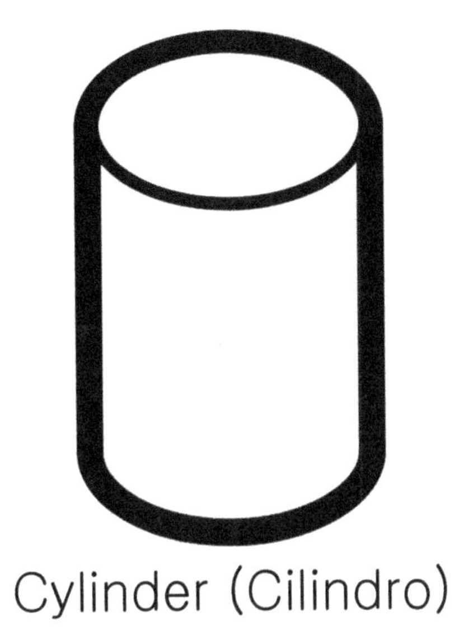

Cylinder (Cilindro)

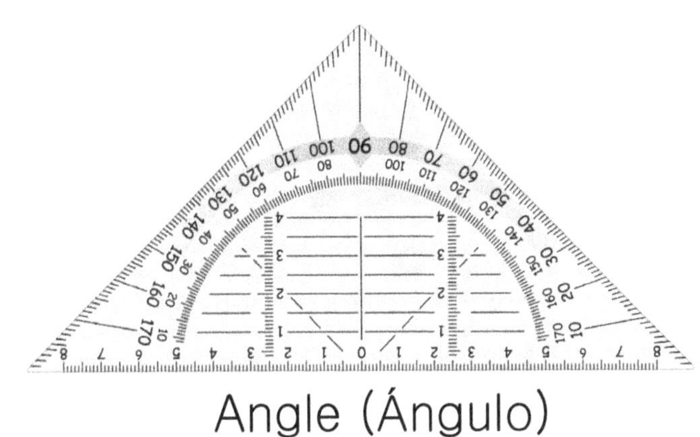

Angle (Ángulo)

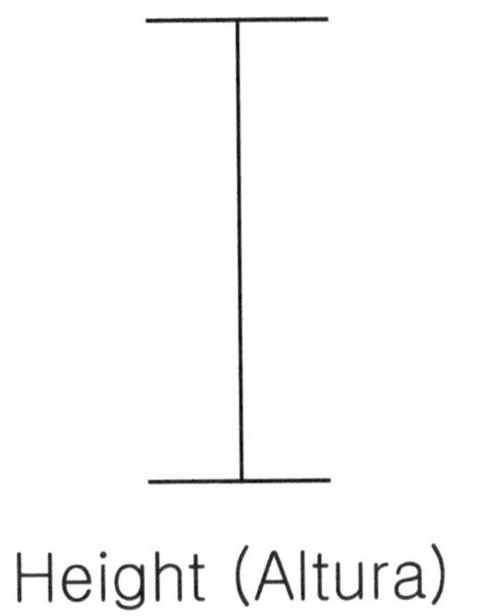

Height (Altura)

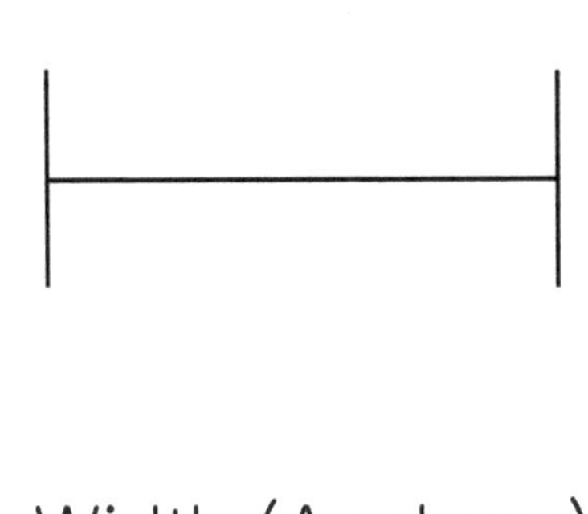

Width (Anchura)

Addition (Adición)

Subtraction (Sustracción)

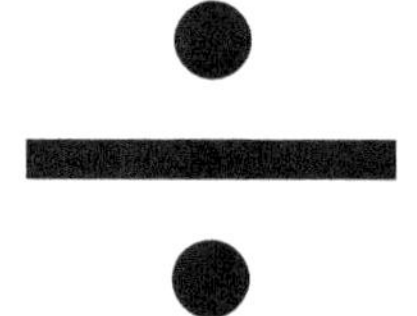

Division (División)

Multiplication (Multiplicación)

Equal Sign (Signo igual)

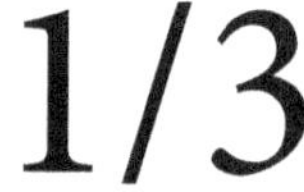

Fraction (Fraction)

Calculator (Calculadora)

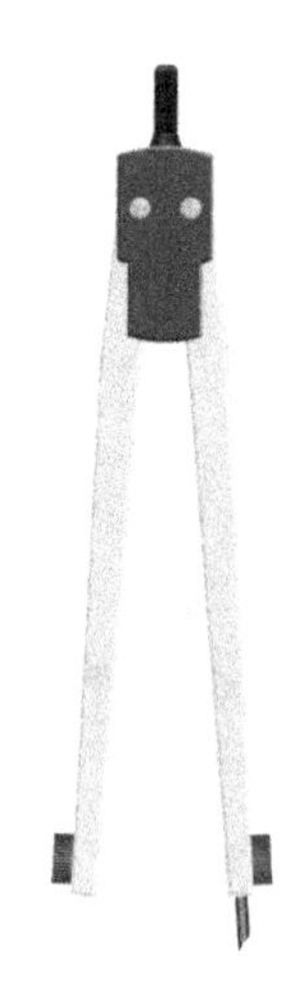

Compass (Compás)

SISTEMA SOLAR(태양계)

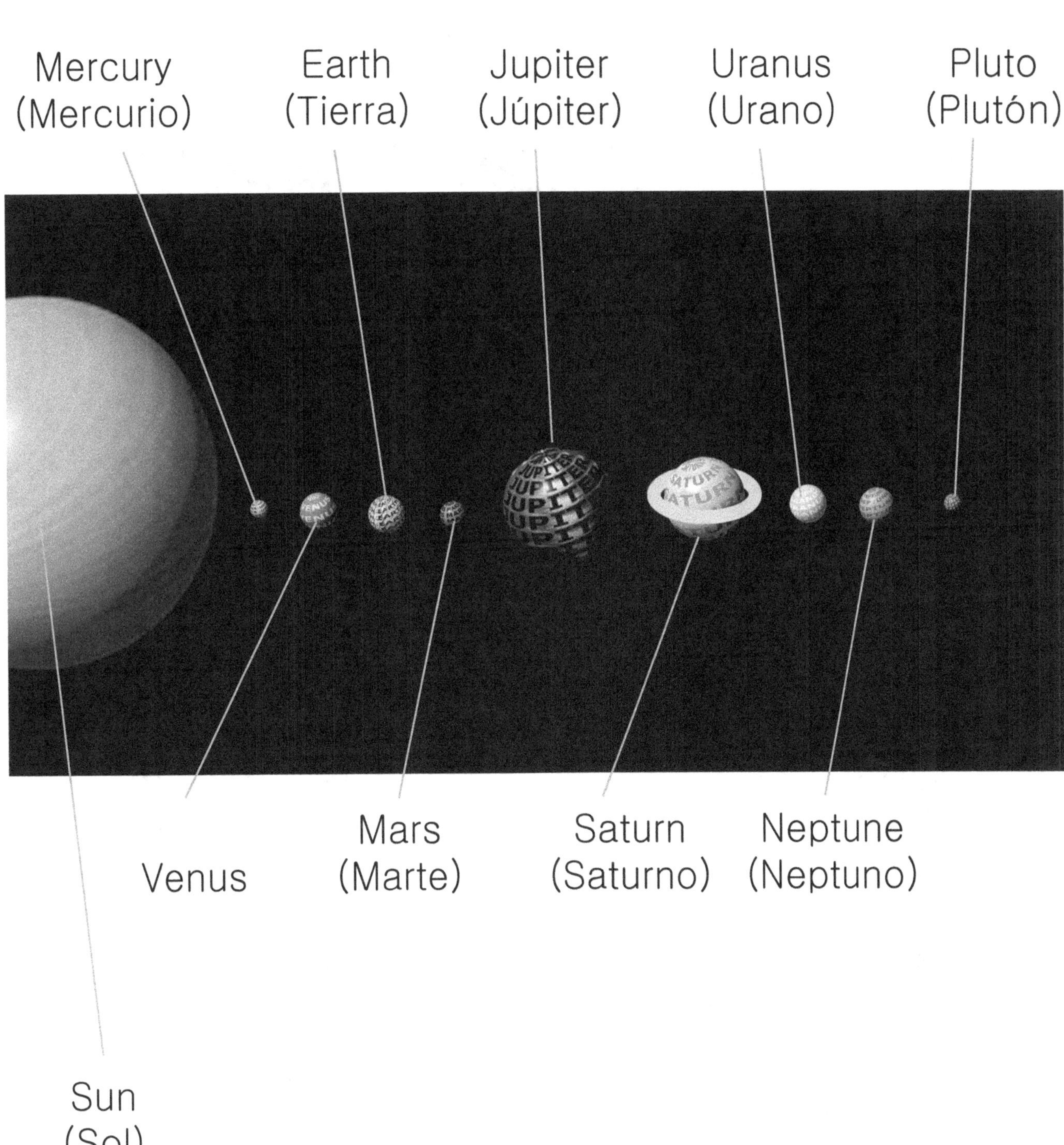

Land
(Tierra)
Cloud
(Nube)
North Pole
(Polo Norte)
Coast
(Costa)
Continent
(Continente)
South Pole
(Polo Sur)
Sea (Mar)
Atmosphere
(Atmósfera)

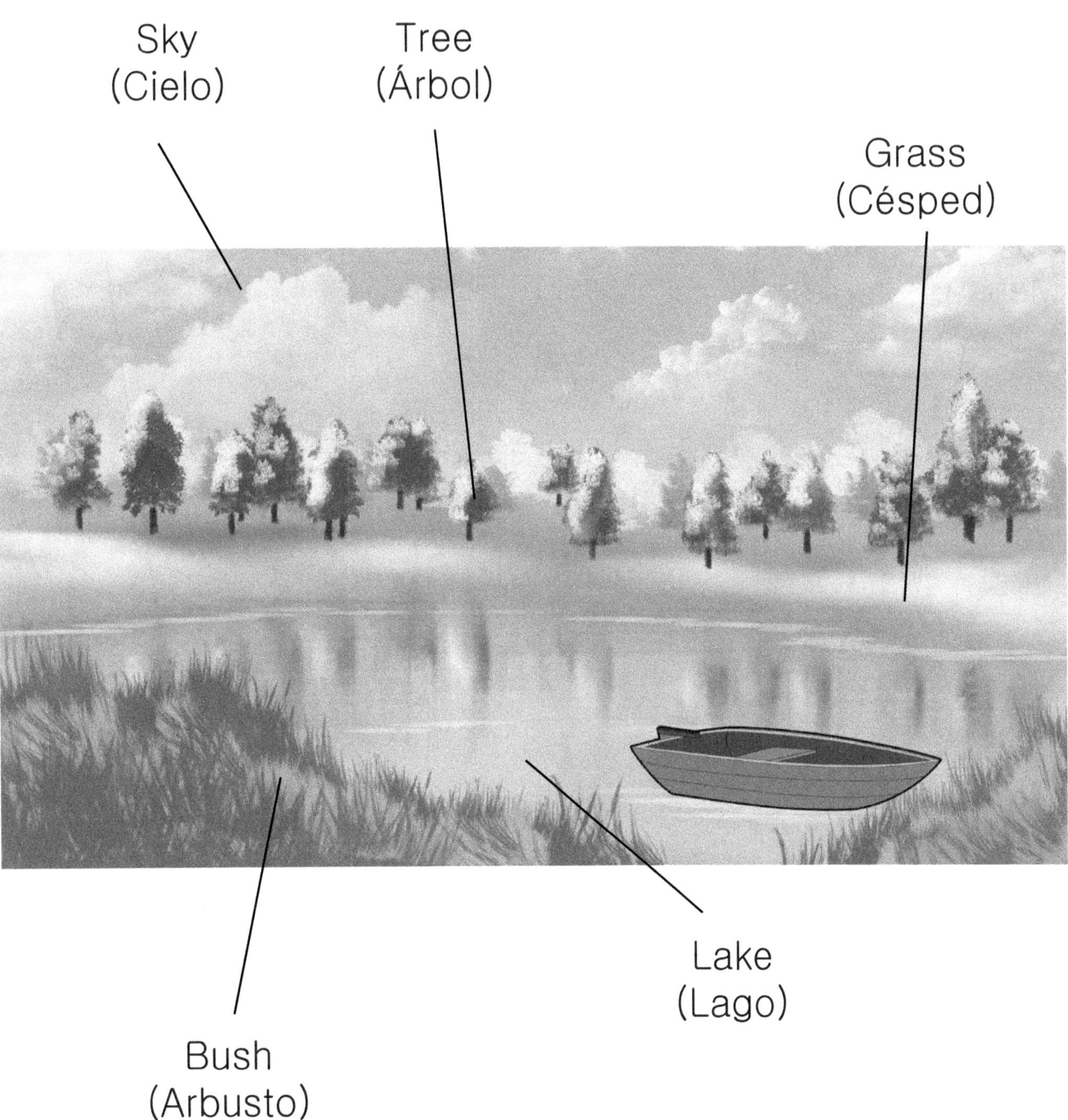

Sky
(Cielo)
Tree
(Árbol)
Grass
(Césped)
Bush
(Arbusto)
Lake
(Lago)

OUTDOORS (AIRE LIBRE)

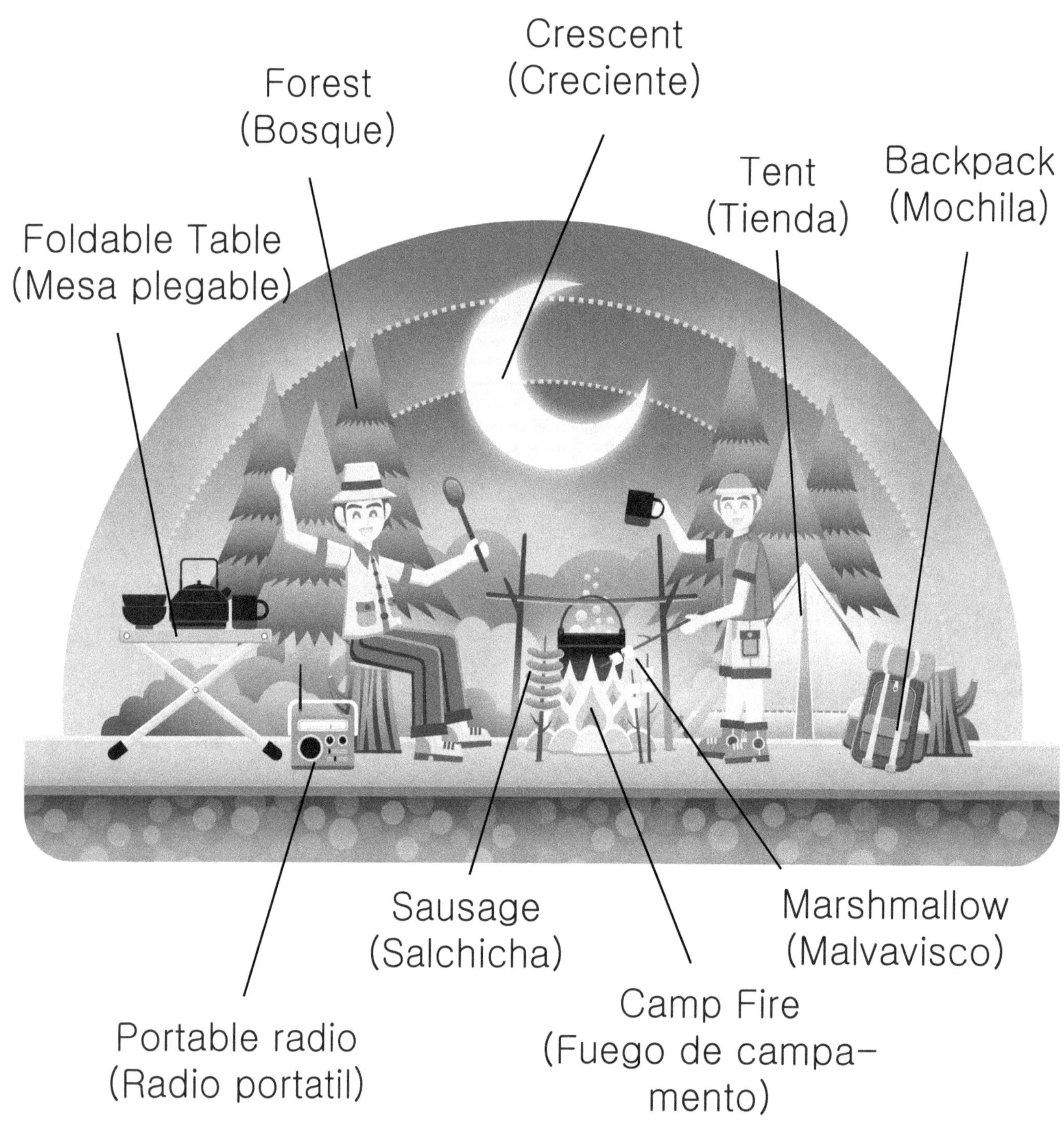

COLORS (COLORES)

Red (Rojo)
Orange (Naranja)
Yellow (Amarillo)
Green (Verde)
Blue (Azul)
Índigo
Violet (Violeta)

APPAREL/ACCESSORIES (ROPA/ACCESSORIOS)

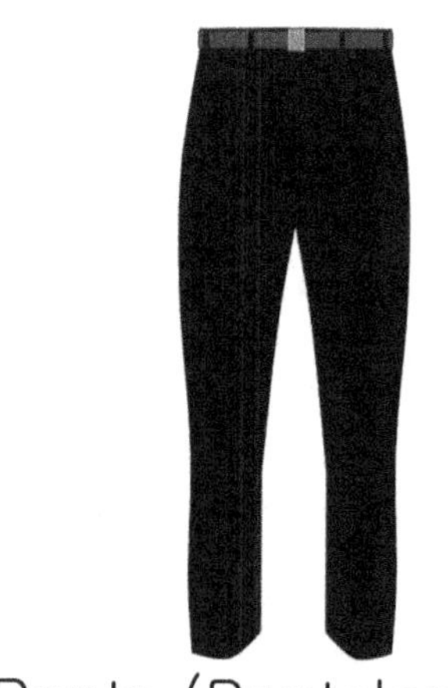

Pants (Pantalones)

Dress Shirt (Camisa de vestir)

T-Shirt

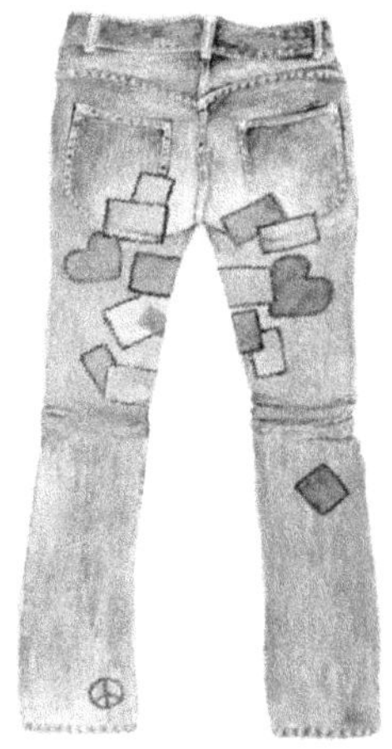

Jeans

Sweatshirt
(Camisa de entrenamiento)

Suit (Traje)

Dress (Vestir)

Jacket (Chaqueta)

Mini Skirt (Minifalda)

Sleepware (Ropa de dormir)

Coat (Capa)

Short Pants
(Pantalones cortos)

Swimsuit
(Traje de baño)

Skirt (Falda)

Cotton Trousers
(Pantalones de algodón)

Polo Shirt (Polo)

Panties (Bragas)

Bra (Sostén)

Hat (Sombrero)

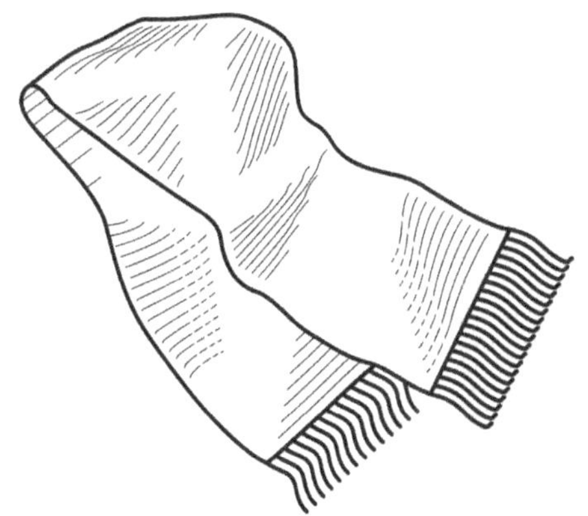

Scarf/Muffler
(Bufanda)

Shoes (Zapatos)

Dress Shoes
(Zapatos de vestir)

Athletic Shoes
(Zapatos atléticos)

Socks (Calcetines)

Bracelet (Pulsera)

Necklace (Collar)

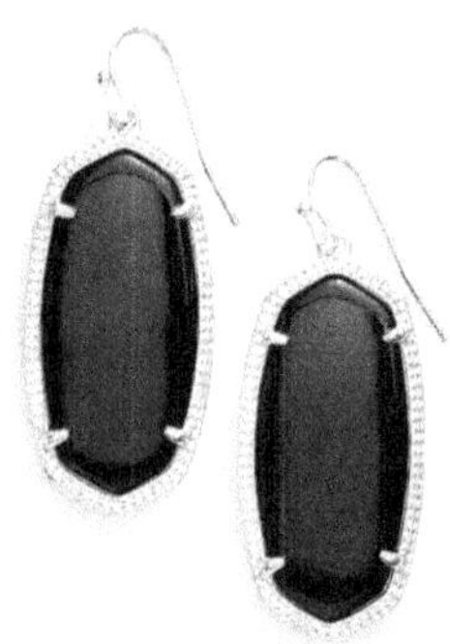

Earring
(Arete)

Ring (Anillo)

Watch (Reloj de mano)

Vest (Chaleco)

Glasses (Gafas)

Sun Glasses
(Gafas de sol)

Slippers
(Zapatillas)

Flip Flops (Chancletas)

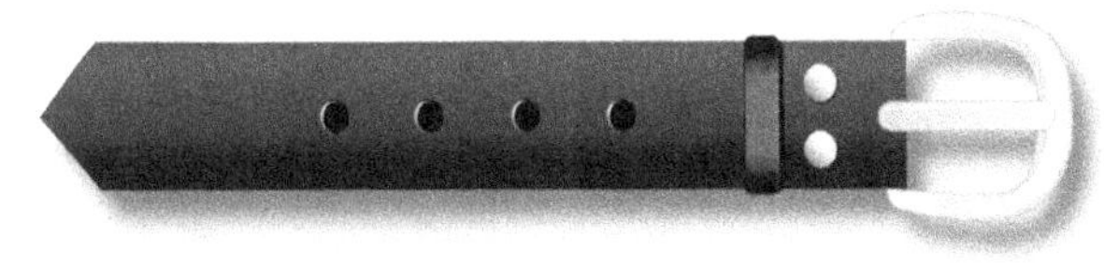

Belt (Cinturón)

Tie (Corbata)

FEMALE PRODUCTS (PRODUCTOS FEMINOS)

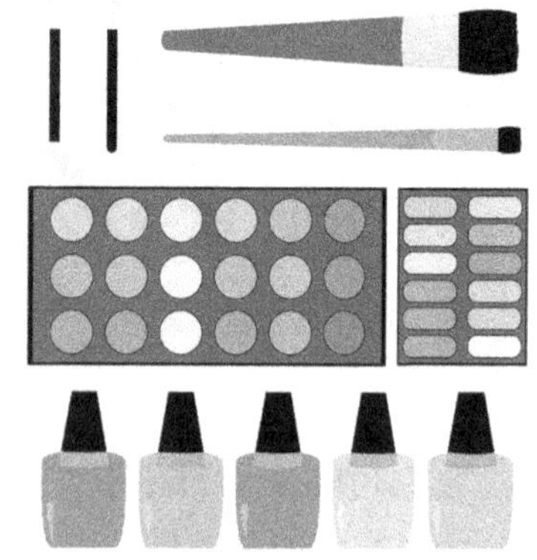

Cosmetics
(Productos cosméticos)

Headband (Vincha)

Sanitary Pad
(Toalla sanitaria)

Face Cleanser
(Limpiador facial)

Mascara (Máscara)

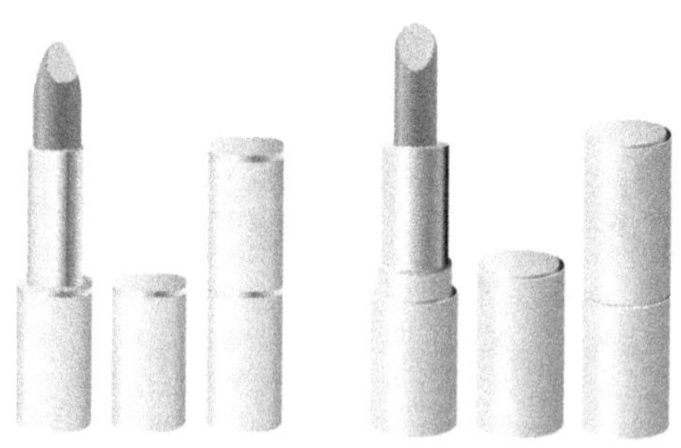

Lipstick (Lápiz labial)

Perfume

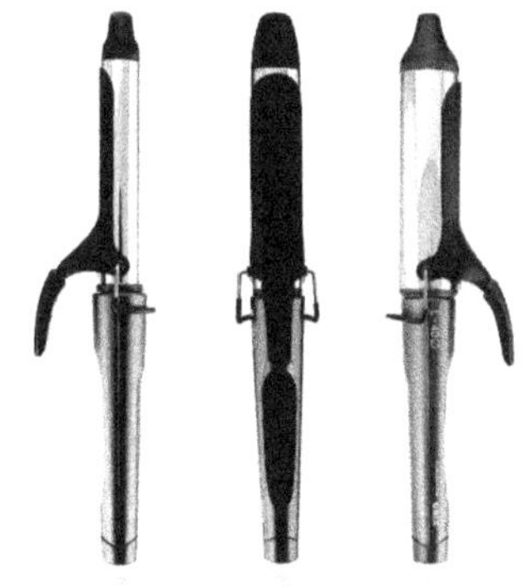

Curling Iron
(Hierro de curling)

Brush (Cepillo)

Wig (Peluca)

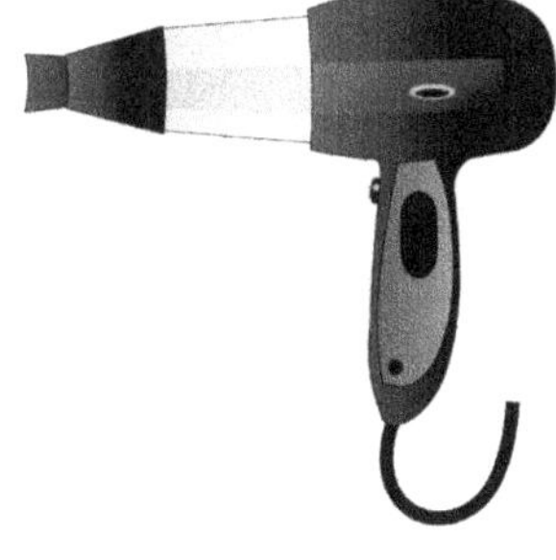

Hair Dryer
(Secador de pelo)

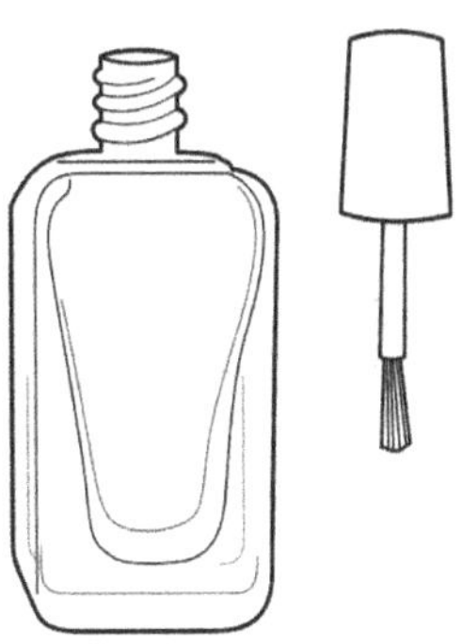

Manicure (Manicura)

MALE PRODUCTS (MALE PRODUCTS)

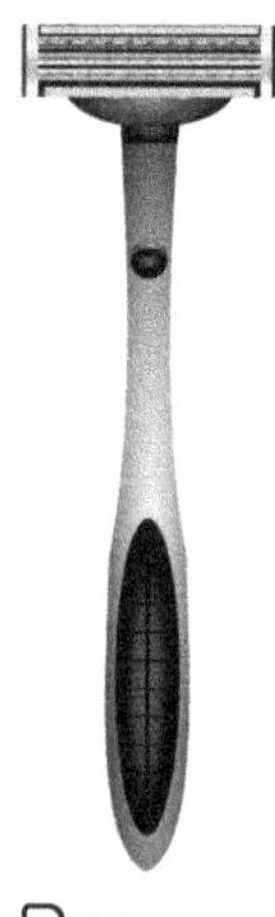

Razor
(Máquina de afeitar)

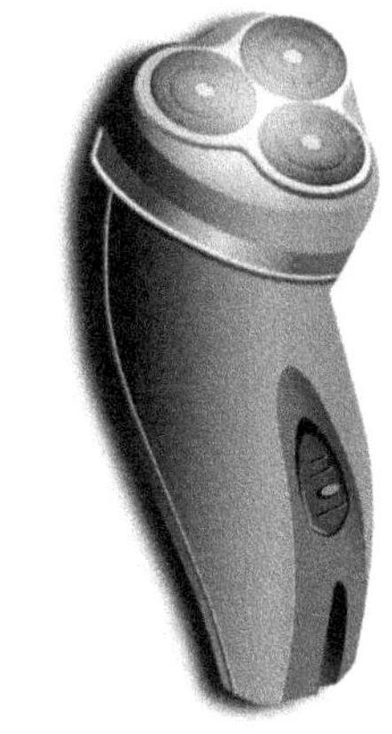

Electric Shaver
(Afeitadora eléctrica)

Cologne (Colonia)

Condom (Condón)

Briefcase (Maletín)

Shoe Horn (Cuerno de zapatos)

RESTAURANT (RESTAURANTE)

Fork (Tenedor)

Knife (Cuchillo)

Chopsticks (Palillos)

Spoon (Cuchara)

Bowl (cuenco)

Rice Bowl (Bol de arroz)

Dish (Plato de comida)

Tablecloth (Mantel)

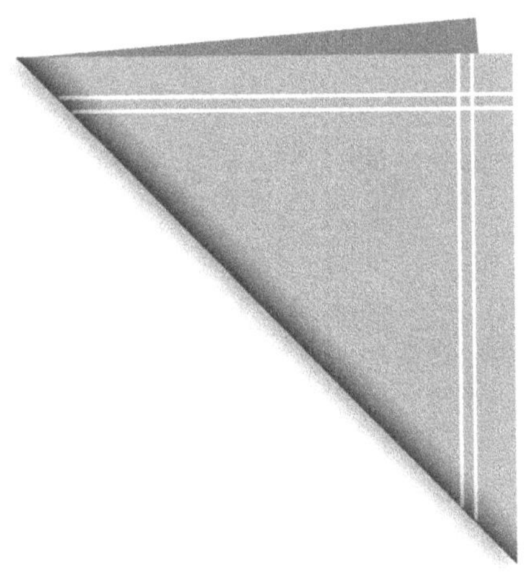

Napkin (Servilleta)

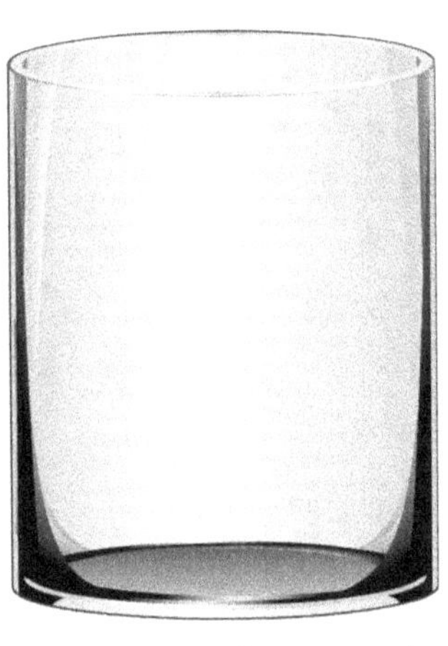

Glass (Vaso)

Sauce (Salsa)

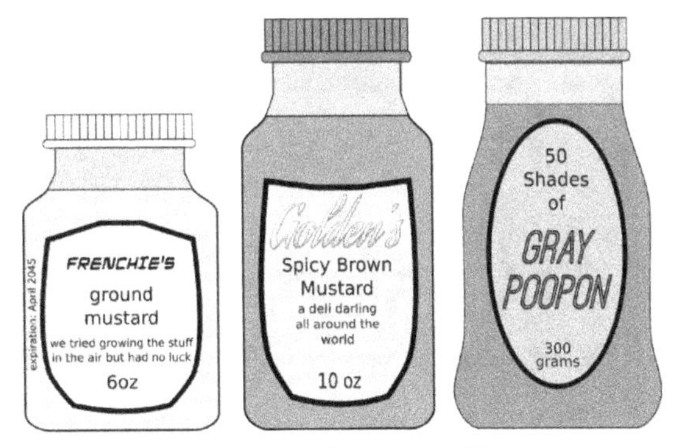

Condiments (Condimentos)

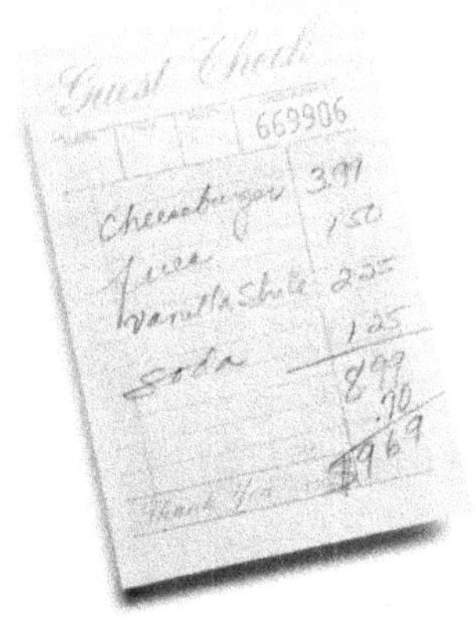

Bill (Cuenta)

Bib (Babero)

Chef/Cook (Cocinero)

Reservation (Reserva)

Order (Orden)

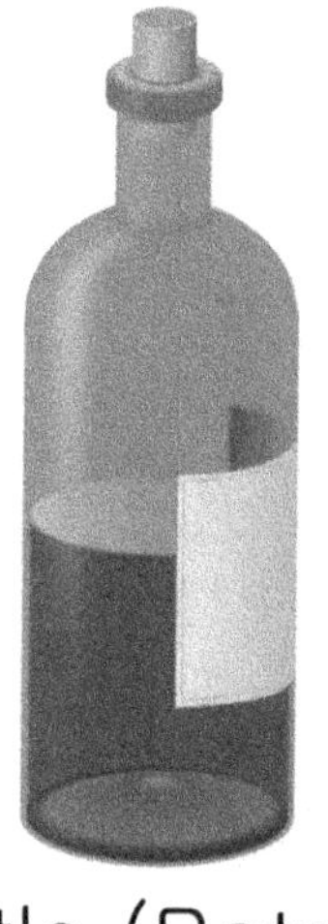

Bottle (Botella)

FOOD/BEVERAGE (COMIDA/BEBIDA)

Cuisine (Cocina)

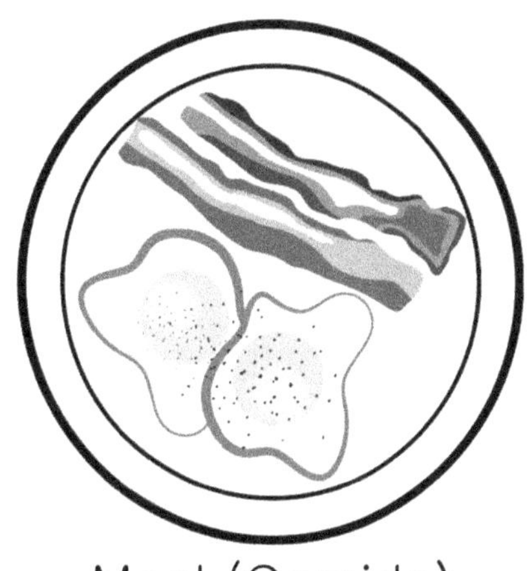

Meal (Comida)

Prix Fixe
(Tabla de hote)

Snack
(Bocadillo)

Box Lunch (Portacomidas)

Whole Chicken (Pollo entero)

Fried Egg (Huevo frito)

Seaweed
(Algas marinas)

Noodles
(Tallarines)

Rice (Arroz)

Side Dishes (Guarniciones)

Grilled Fish (Pescado asado)

Coffee (café)

Tea (Té)

Sports Drinks
(Bebidas deportivas)

Milk (Leche)

Coca

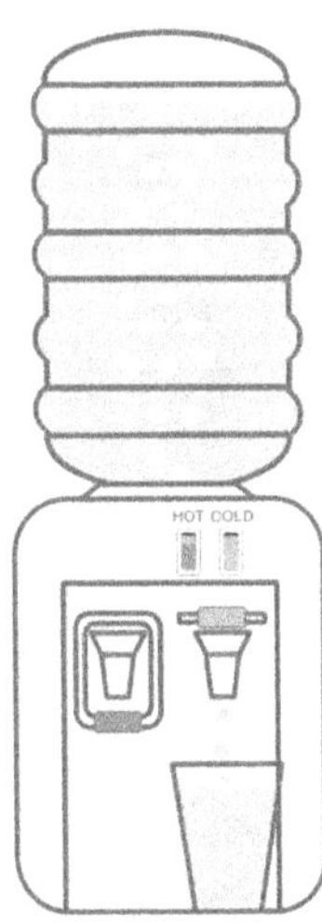

Water (Agua)

Ice Water
(Agua congelada)

Juice (Jugo)

Sparkling Water
(Agua con gas)

Beer (Cerveza)

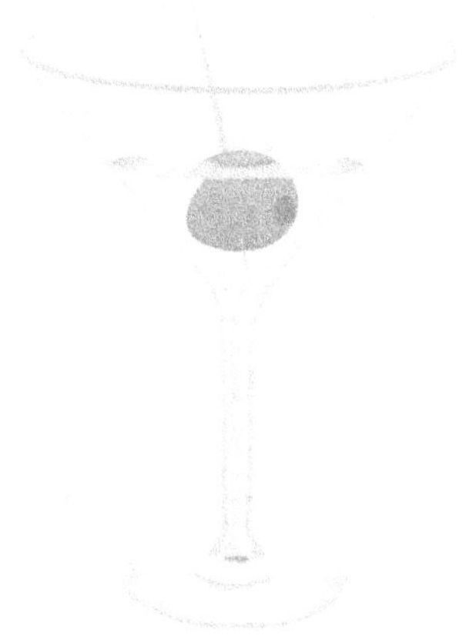

Alcoholic Drinks
(Bebida alcoholica)

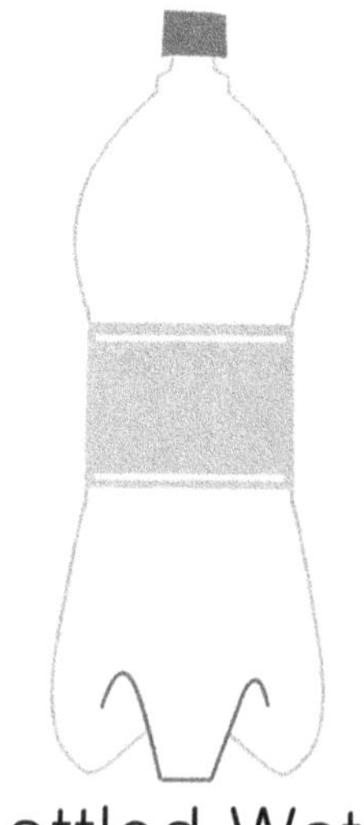

Bottled Water
(Agua embotellada)

CALENDAR(CALENDARIO)

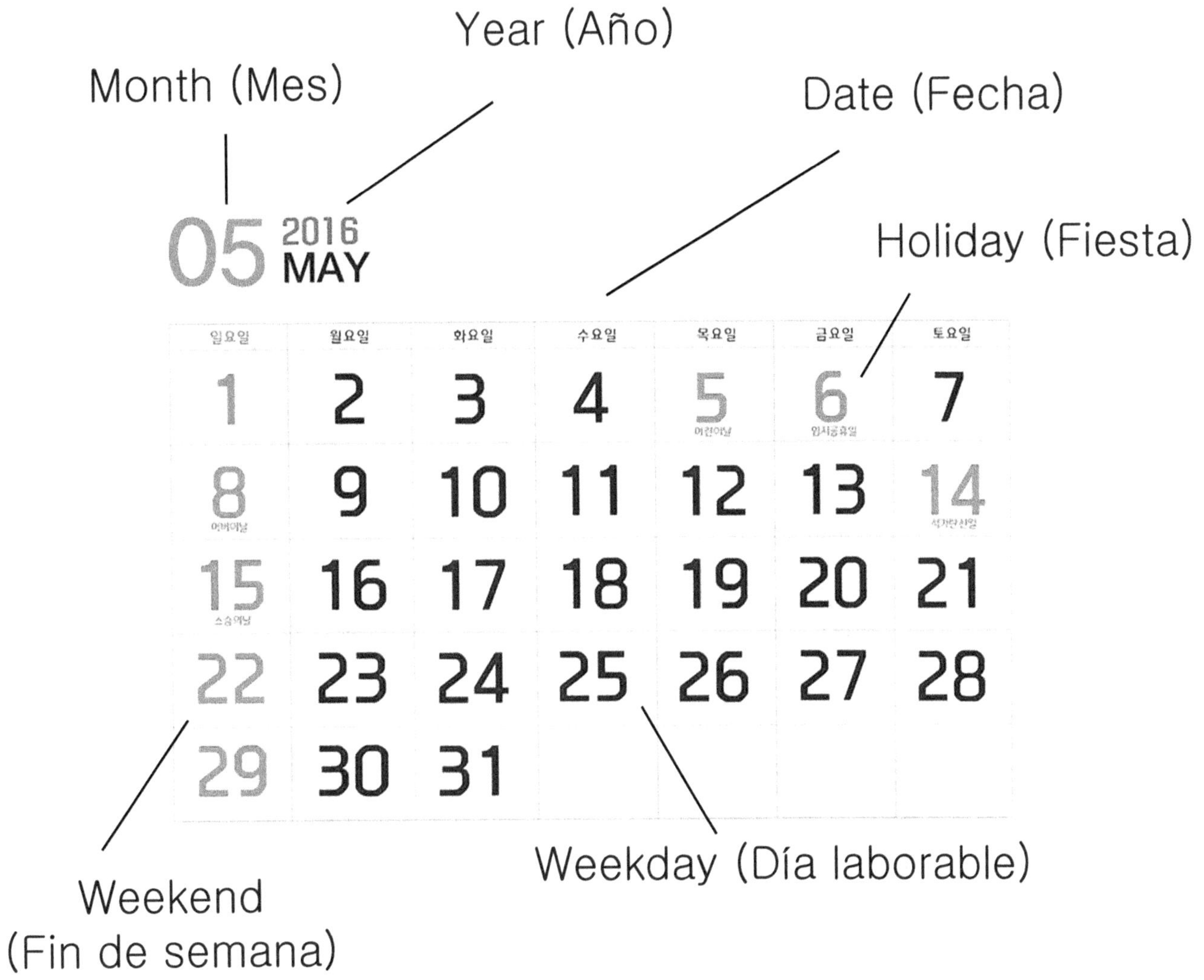

Monday (Lunes) Tuesday (Martes)

Wednesday (Miércoles) Thursday (Jueves)

Friday (Viernes) Saturday (Sábado) Sunday (Domingo)

SEASONS/WEATHER
(ESTACIONES/TIEMPO)

Spring (Primavera)　　　Summer (Verano)

Fall/Autumn (Otoño)　　　Winter (Invierno)

Cloudy (Nublado)

Sunny (Soleado)

Thunder and Lightning
(Truenos y relámpagos)

Hail (Granizo)

Snow (Nieve)

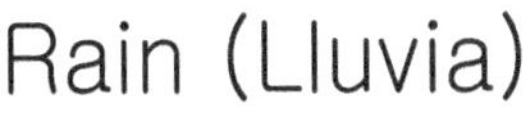

Rain (Lluvia)

Strong Wind
(Viento fuerte)

Fine Dust (Polvo fino)

Summer Monsoon
(Las lluvias)

Drought (Sequía)

Flood (Inundar)

Heavy Snow
(Fuertes nevadas)

Earthquake
(Terremoto)

Volcano Erruption
(Erupción volcánica)

Tsunami

Landslide
(Deslizamiento de tierra)

Avalanche (Avalancha)

Tornado (Tifón)

PLACES (LUGARES)

Post Office
(Oficina postal)

Police Station
(Estación de policía)

Library (Biblioteca)

Firestation (Estación de bomberos)

Department Store
(Grandes almacenes)

Park (Parque)

Karaoke

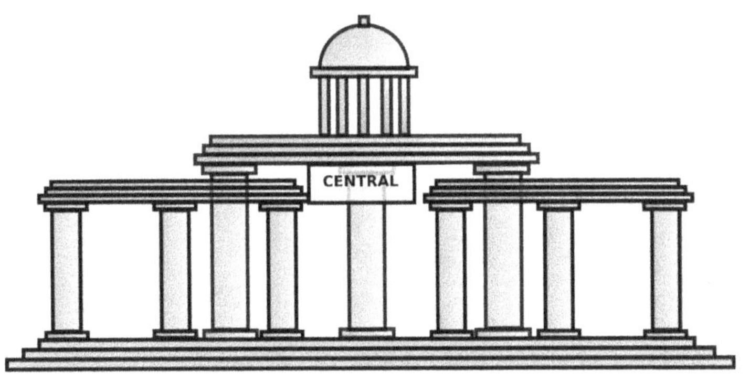

City Hall
(Palacio Municipal)

Hospital

Bank (Banco)

Theater (Cine)

Church (Iglesia)

Beach (Playa)

Bus Stop
(Parada de autobús)

Zoo

Museum (Museo)

Playground
(Patio de recreo)

Amusement Park
(Parque de atracciones)

Gas Station
(Gasolinera)

Convenience Store
(Tienda de conveniencia)

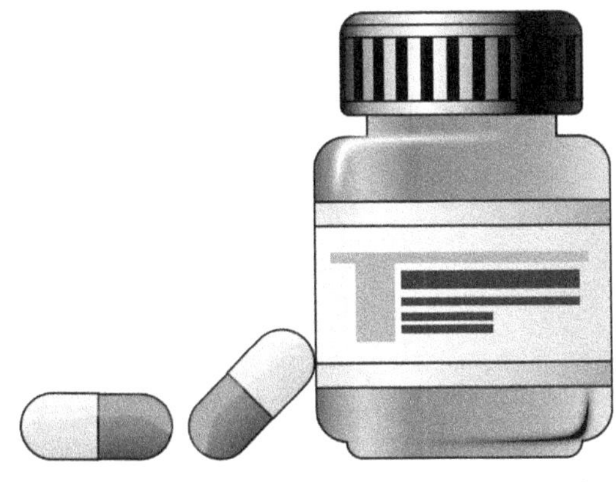

Pharmacy (Farmacia)

Emergency Room
(Sala de emergencias)

Spa/Sauna

Bakery (Panadería)

THINGS (COSAS)

Post Stamps
(Sello de correos)

Envelope (Sobre)

Handcuffs (Esposas)

Pistol (Pistola)

Vault (Caja Fuerte)

Librarian (Bibliotecario)

Fire Extinguisher
(Extintor de incendios)

Firetruck
(Camión de bomberos)

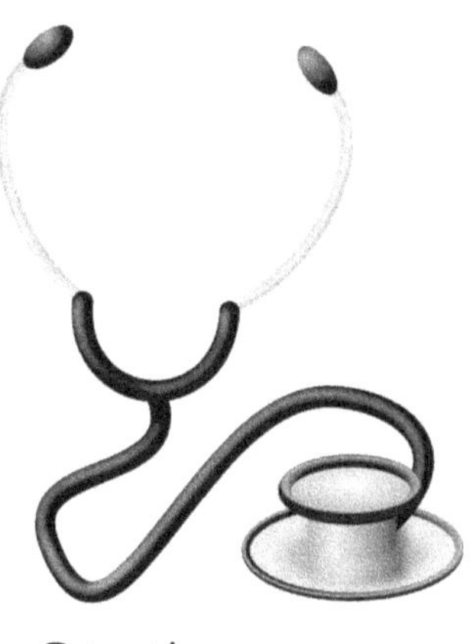

Stethoscope
(Estetoscopio)

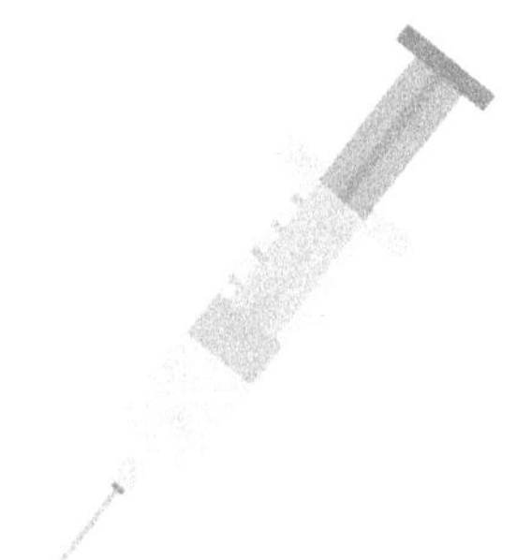

Syringe (Jeringuilla)

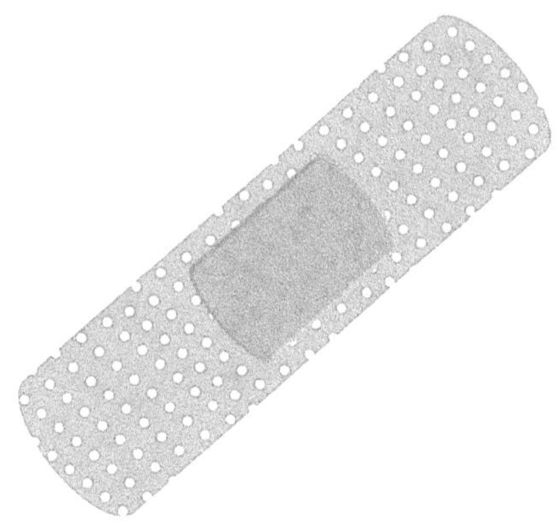

Band Aid (Tirita)

Patient (Paciente)

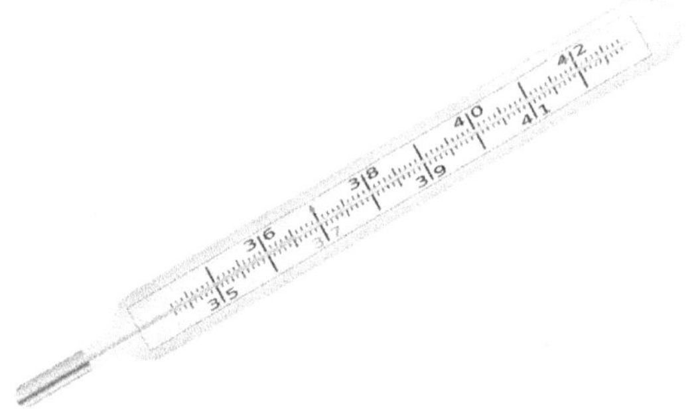

Thermometer (Termómetro)

Ointment (Ungüento)

Father (Padre)

Nun (Monja)

Communion (Comunión)

Cross (Cruz)

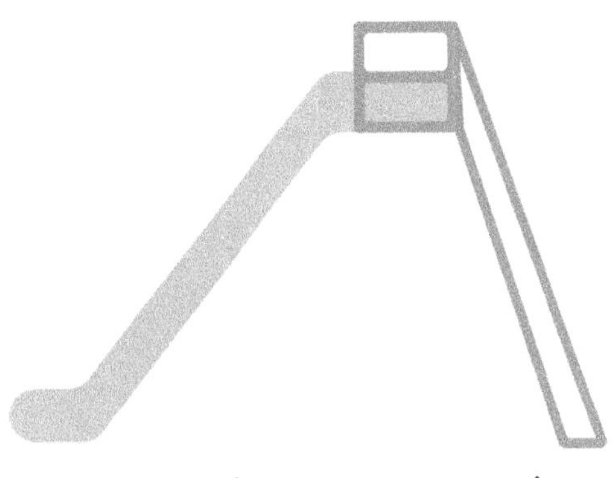

Slide (Tobogán   )

Swing (Columpio)

Banker (Banquero)

Paper Bill (Papel moneda)

Coin (Acuñar)

Gasoline (Gasolina)